CHUNK
POTATO CHIPS
BUZZ COLA
CANNED MEAT

BART SIMPSON™
SON OF HOMER

TITAN BOOKS

BART SIMPSON: SON OF HOMER

Collects Bart Simpson Comics 29, 30, 31, 32, 33

Published in the UK by Titan Books, a division of Titan Publishing Group,
144 Southwark St., London SE1 0UP, under licence from Bongo Entertainment, Inc.

FIRST EDITION: MARCH 2009

ISBN 9781848562288

4 6 8 10 9 7 5 3

Publisher: Matt Groening
Creative Director: Bill Morrison
Managing Editor: Terry Delegeane
Director of Operations: Robert Zaugh
Art Director: Nathan Kane
Art Director Special Projects: Serban Cristescu
Production Manager: Christopher Ungar
Assistant Art Director: Chia-Hsien Jason Ho
Production/Design: Karen Bates, Nathan Hamill, Art Villanueva
Staff Artist: Mike Rote
Administration: Sherri Smith, Pete Benson
Legal Guardian: Susan A. Grode

Trade Paperback Concepts and Design: Serban Cristescu

Cover: Ryan Rivette, Dan Davis and Serban Cristescu

Contributing Artists:
Karen Bates, Jeff Brennan, John Costanza, Serban Cristescu, Mike DeCarlo, John Delaney,
Nathan Hamill, Jason Ho, James Lloyd, Nathan Kane, Bill Morrison, Joey Nilges, Phyllis Novin,
Phil Ortiz, Andrew Pepoy, Ryan Rivette, Mike Rote, Howard Shum, Chris Ungar, Art Villanueva

Contributing Writers:
James W. Bates, Tony DiGerolamo, Evan Dorkin, Amanda McCann,
Jesse Leon McCann, Tom Peyer, Eric Rogers, Mary Trainor

PRINTED IN SPAIN

CONTENTS

6 ROOFTOP REPAIR
7 BART COPS OUT
17 IF YOU CAN'T WIGGUM, JOIN 'EM
19 K-BART
31 THE BOOK THAT ATE SPRINGFIELD
43 THE SECRET LIFE OF BART SIMPSON
47 THE GREAT TRAIN WRECK
56 DIGGING A HOLE
57 SPREE FOR ALL
69 HANDY POP CULTURE QUOTES FOR ALL OCCASIONS
71 SHOPPING FOR SCHOOL SUPPLIES THE BART SIMPSON WAY
73 THE MAGGIE & MOE MYSTERIES: THE DISAPPEARING DUCHESS
82 WORKER AND PARASITE
83 HOG TIED
91 CLONE ALONE
98 BABY GOT BACK AT BURNS
108 FORT KNOCKS
115 THE UTER BOMBER

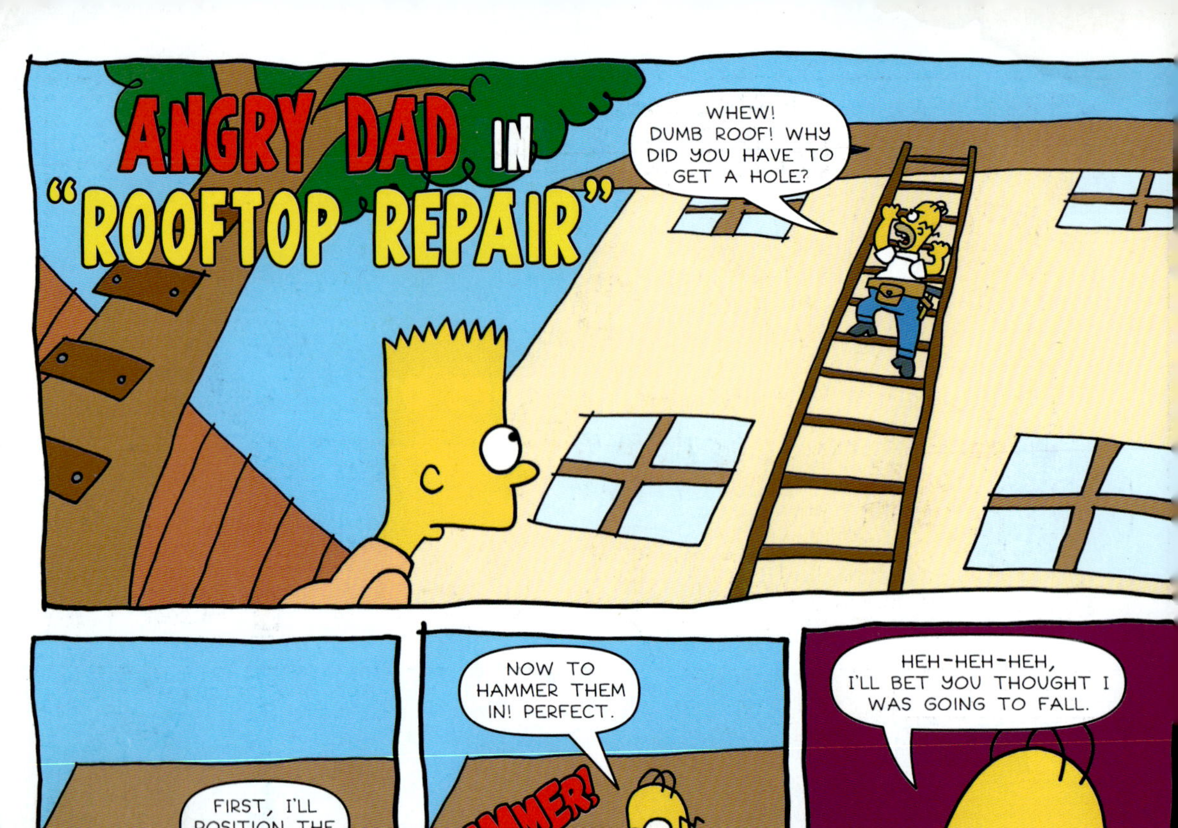

TONY DIGEROLAMO SCRIPT · JASON HO PENCILS & INKS · NATHAN HAMILL COLORS · KAREN BATES LETTERS

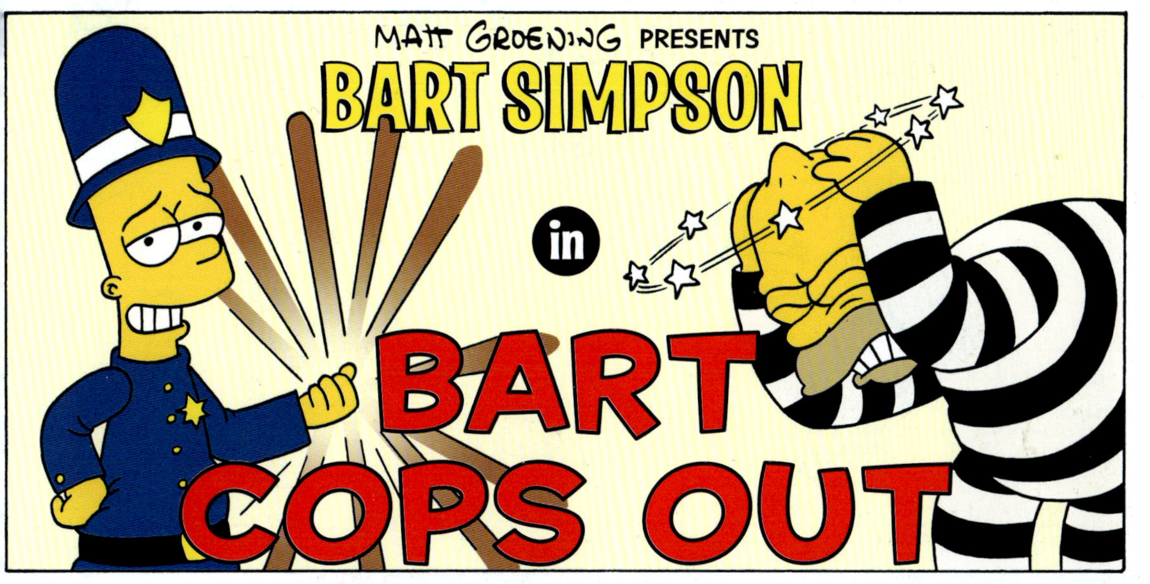

MATT GROENING PRESENTS

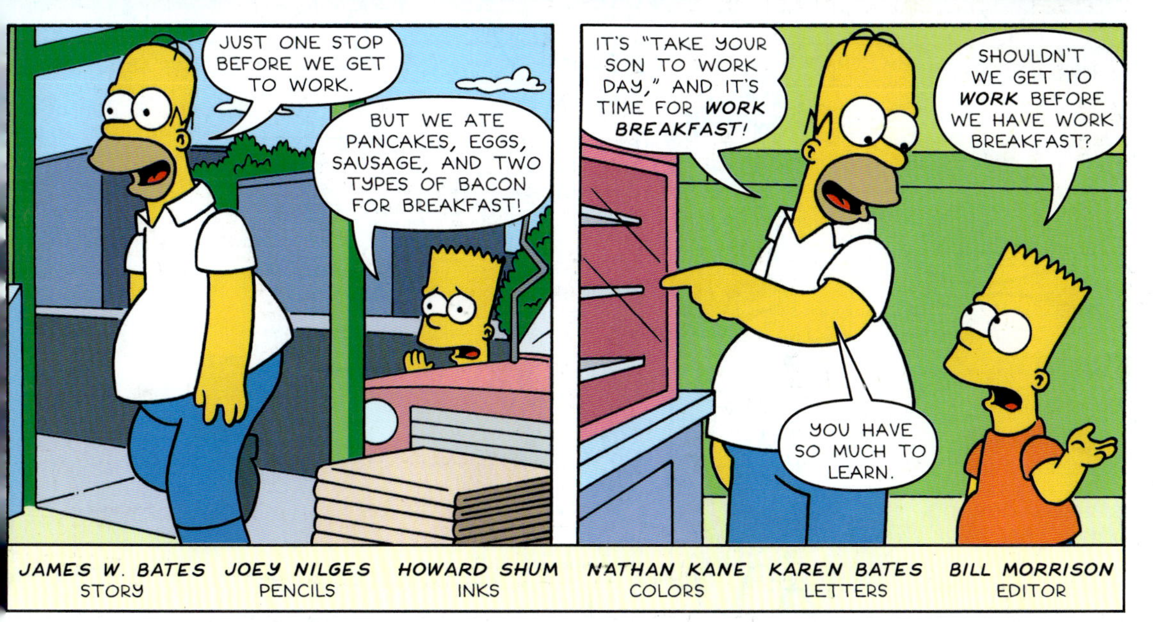

EARLY ONE MORNING...

JUST ONE STOP BEFORE WE GET TO WORK.
BUT WE ATE PANCAKES, EGGS, SAUSAGE, AND TWO TYPES OF BACON FOR BREAKFAST!
IT'S "TAKE YOUR SON TO WORK DAY," AND IT'S TIME FOR WORK BREAKFAST!
SHOULDN'T WE GET TO WORK BEFORE WE HAVE WORK BREAKFAST?
YOU HAVE SO MUCH TO LEARN.

JAMES W. BATES STORY
JOEY NILGES PENCILS
HOWARD SHUM INKS
NATHAN KANE COLORS
KAREN BATES LETTERS
BILL MORRISON EDITOR

D'OH. ONLY ONE LEFT.

AND IT'S MINE.

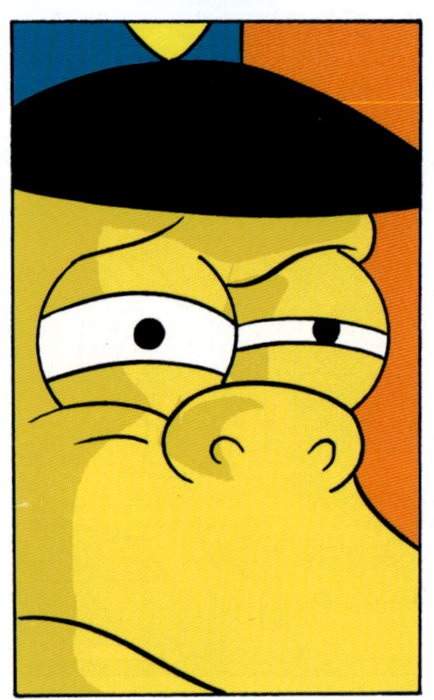

HM...THAT WORKS.
SORRY, FOR THE HASSLE. I'M STRESSED OUT. IT'S THIS "TAKE YOUR SON TO WORK DAY."

ME, TOO. I LOVE MY RALPHIE, BUT HE RIDES ON PATROL WITH ME ALL THE TIME.
TELL ME ABOUT IT. LIKE I NEED TO SPEND MORE TIME WITH ***THE BOY***.

HEY, I'VE GOT AN IDEA. WHY DON'T YOU TAKE RALPHIE FOR THE DAY, AND I'LL TAKE BART.
YOU'LL TAKE BART? HMM...

I'LL TAKE BART, BUT REMEMBER...YOU GET RALPHIE.
MY HAIR IS TINGLY.
TRY NOT TO BREATHE IN, MAN.

IT'D BE GOOD TO KNOW THAT BART IS IN POLICE CUSTODY. IT'S A DEAL! ***TAKE MY KID TO WORK!***
ANYWAY, WHAT HARM CAN RALPHIE DO AT A FANCY SAFE-GUARDED NUCLEAR PLANT?

COOL! THERE'S A NEW SHERIFF IN TOWN.
I LIKE THE NUC-U-LAR PLANTS WITH YELLOW LEAVES.

LATER THAT DAY...
SO, BART. WHAT WOULD YOU LIKE TO KNOW ABOUT BEING A POLICEMAN?
HOW MUCH CASH DO YOU STUFF IN YOUR POCKETS WHEN YOU CATCH A BANK ROBBER?
WELL, I...
WHEN YOU BEAT UP A PERP, HOW DO KEEP HIM FROM BRUISING?

BART YOUR QUESTIONS ARE HARD TO ANSWER.
WHY? IS THE TOPIC OF ***POLICE CORRUPTION*** TOO HOT TO HANDLE?
NO. I'M GETTING CHOKED UP. RALPH ISN'T HALF THIS INTERESTED IN WHAT I ***REALLY*** DO.

MR. BART'S DAD, MY BELT BUCKLE IS GLOWY.
THAT'S WHAT WE CALL RADIATION! IF YOU LIKE THAT, YOU SHOULD SEE THE UTENSILS IN THE CAFETERIA.

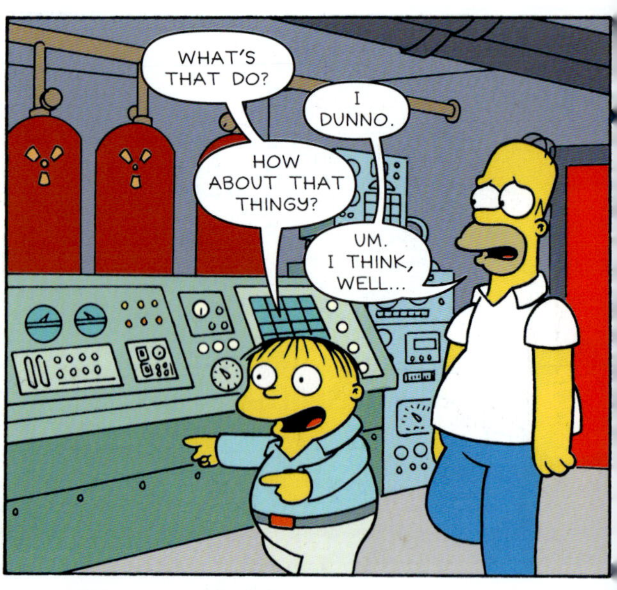
WHAT'S THAT DO?
I DUNNO.
HOW ABOUT THAT THINGY?
UM. I THINK, WELL...

CAN I TOUCH THAT?
YOU PROBABLY SHOULDN'T.
TOXIC

THE VOICES BETWEEN MY EARS SAY I SHOULD TOUCH IT.
WHY DON'T WE GO TOUCH THE SODA MACHINE INSTEAD.

MEANWHILE, ON THE BEAT...
...AND THAT'S WHY MOST OF THE CRIMINALS ON TELEVISION DON'T WEAR SHIRTS.
I'M LEARNING SO MUCH.

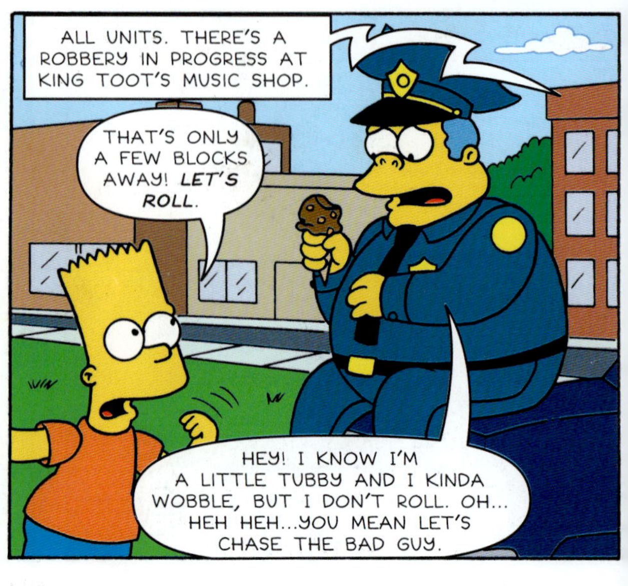
ALL UNITS. THERE'S A ROBBERY IN PROGRESS AT KING TOOT'S MUSIC SHOP.
THAT'S ONLY A FEW BLOCKS AWAY! LET'S ROLL.
HEY! I KNOW I'M A LITTLE TUBBY AND I KINDA WOBBLE, BUT I DON'T ROLL. OH... HEH HEH...YOU MEAN LET'S CHASE THE BAD GUY.

THIS IS PRETTY COOL.
WOO-WOO-WOO!

WHEN YOU SEE HOW LOW THESE MARCHING BAND JUNKIES WILL STOOP FOR A FIX, IT REALLY HITS A SOUR NOTE.
KING TOOT'

THE THIEF MUST HAVE A LOOSE SPIT VALVE. I'VE FOUND A TRAIL LEADING THIS WAY.

THAT'S REALLY GROSS BUT GOOD DETECTIVE WORK, BART. YOU'RE THE ***BEST PARTNER*** I'VE EVER HAD.
THANKS.

C'MON, BART. LET'S FIND THIS PERP.
DON'T YOU THINK IT'S TIME TO GIVE ME A GUN?

I CAN'T GIVE YOU A GUN.
AW C'MON, MAN. YOU CAN TRUST ME.
IT'S NOT THAT. I ***LOST*** MY EXTRA GUN SOMEWHERE AND CAN'T FIND IT! I EVEN CHECKED UNDER THE COUCH CUSHIONS.

CAN I PRESS THIS ONE?
NO.
CAN I PRESS THIS ONE?
NO.
THIS ONE?
NO.

HERE, PLAY WITH THIS KNOB. I THINK IT FELL OFF LAST WEEK.

THIS LOLLIPOP TASTES LIKE MOMMY'S SHOES.

REACTOR CORE MELTDOWN!
BEEP!
BEEP! BEEP!
BEEP!
MELTDOWN?! OH, WHY DOES THIS KEEP HAPPENING ON MY SHIFT?
BEEP! BEEP! BEEP!

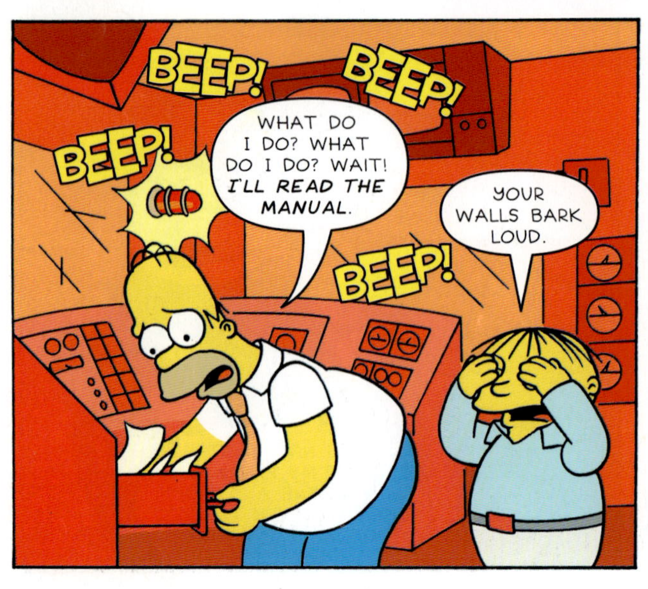
BEEP!
BEEP!
BEEP!
WHAT DO I DO? WHAT DO I DO? WAIT! I'LL READ THE MANUAL.
BEEP!
YOUR WALLS BARK LOUD.

WHY DIDN'T I LISTEN TO LENNY WHEN HE TOLD ME NOT TO USE A FRUIT ROLL-UP AS A BOOK MARK?
WARNING! MELTDOWN IMMINENT
BEEP!
BEEP!
BEEP!
BEEP!

THE SUN HAS GONE DOWN ON THE CITY STREETS OF SPRINGFIELD...

DUDE, I DIDN'T ROB THAT MUSIC STORE!
YOU'RE CARRYING A BASSOON.

SMELL YA LATER, SLOWPOKES.

HUFF! HUFF! I GUESS WE LOST HIM.

NO ONE CAN RUN THAT QUICK CARRYING A MASSIVE WOODWIND LIKE THAT. HE MUST HAVE GONE DOWN THIS ALLEY.

I KNOW THIS ALLEY. I COME HERE SOMETIMES WHEN THE BULLIES WANT TO BEAT ME UP. THERE'S A HIDING SPOT RIGHT HERE!
El Barto

FREEZE!
I KNEW IT!

BOOK 'EM, BART-O.
BUMMER. ALL I WANTED TO DO WAS MAKE SOME **BEAUTIFUL MUSIC**.

YOU DID GOOD TODAY, BART.
THANKS. HAVING UNJUSTIFIED YET EASILY ABUSED POWER IS FUN.

YOU THINK YOU WANNA BE A COP WHEN YOU GET OLDER?
ARE YOU KIDDING? IF I WASN'T THERE, YOU NEVER WOULD HAVE CAUGHT HIM. I CAN SEE A ***LUCRATIVE FUTURE*** IN CRIME IN THIS TOWN.

I WONDER HOW HOMER AND RALPHIE ARE DOING?

IF I REMEMBER MY TRAINING RIGHT, WE'RE EITHER ABOUT TO BECOME SHRIVELED UP ZOMBIES OR 50-FOOT TALL GOLIATHS.

I CAN'T FIGURE OUT HOW TO TURN OFF THE REACTOR.
BEEP!
BEEP!
BEEP!
BEEP!
WHY DON'T YOU TURN *EVERYTHING* OFF? *I KNOW HOW*.

BEEP!
BEEP!
YOU DO?
BEEP!
IT'S EASY. SOMETIMES I TURN OFF MY WHOLE HOUSE.
BEEP!

BEEP!
BEEP!
BEEP!
BEEP!
BEEP!
BEEP!
BEEP!
FIRST, YOU CATCH A PIXIE.
WE'RE *SO* DEAD.

THEN YOU WRAP IT IN TIN FOIL AND PUT IT IN THE MICROWAVE. IT GETS ZAPPY AND THEN THE HOUSE TURNS OFF.
THAT'S IT, YOU BRILLIANT LITTLE WEIRDO! *WE'LL BLOW THE FUSE*.
ONE MINUTE UNTIL CORE MELTDOWN.
BEEP!
BEEP!
BEEP!
BEEP!

AND MARGE SAID I'D NEVER USE THE BREAD-O-MATIC AT WORK.
BEEP!
BEEP!
WHERE'S THE PIXIE?
BEEP!
BEEP!
BEEP!
BREAD-O-MATIC

LET'S HOPE THIS IS ENOUGH TO OVERLOAD THE FUSE!
BEEP!
BEEP!
BEEP!
BEEP!

CLICK!
WOO-HOO! IT WORKED!
EMERGENCY POWER INITIATED. CORE RETURNING TO NORMAL.

IS EVERY-THING DUCKY? I THOUGHT I HEARD AN ALARM.
AAAH! A SHRIVELED ZOMBIE!

LATER, AT THE KWIK-E-MART...
YOU SHOULDA SEEN BART. HE TOOK DOWN THAT PERP LIKE A PRO.
AND RALPH'S QUICK THINKING SAVED THE DAY.

WOW, TO THINK MY RALPHIE'S A HERO FOR USING HIS NOGGIN...
...OR THAT BART PREVENTED A CRIME.

THANK YOU, HOMER. YOU'VE SHOWN ME A SIDE OF RALPHIE I NEVER KNEW.
THANK YOU. IT'S NOT OFTEN THAT THE BOY DOES SOMETHING THAT MAKES ME PROUD. WE'VE GOT GOOD KIDS.
YEAH, GOOD AND SMART.

IT'S A DEAL. MY TREASURED OLD BASSOON FOR YOUR COOL GLOW-IN-THE-DARK BELT BUCKLE.
BASSOONS ARE MY FAVORITE KIND OF MONKEY.
THE END

CHIEF WIGGUM & RALPH IN:
IF YOU CAN'T WIGGUM, JOIN 'EM!
YOUR FIRST BASEBALL GAME! ARE YOU AS EXCITED AS I AM, RALPHIE?
'CAUSE IF YOU ARE, WE'D BETTER FIND THE LITTLE BOYS' ROOM!
SPRINGFIELD ISOTOPES vs. SHELBYVILLE VISITORS
I'M AN INDIAN CHIEF!
GOTCHA. NO RUSH ON THE BOYS' ROOM.
KENT BROCKMAN PHOTO DAY (KIDS UNDER 12)
#1
TICKET

HOW ABOUT A HOT DOG, SON?
HOT DOGS
MOMMY MASHES MINE IN MILK!

OKAY, LITTLE BUDDY! SHOW YOUR COLORS!
IF I CLOSE MY EYES, I'M STILL DRESSED!
ISOTOPE
S

TOM PEYER SCRIPT
JAMES LLOYD PENCILS
ANDREW PEPOY INKS
NATHAN HAMILL COLORS
KAREN BATES LETTERS
BILL MORRISON EDITOR

NOW REMEMBER, RALPH. THE MAN WITH THE BAT JUST HITS BALLS, NOT LITTLE BOYS!
THIS MITTEN'S TOO BIG!

HEY, LOOK UP THERE, SON!
AHHH! THIS IS A CREEPY RESTAURANT!

NINE INNINGS LATER...
LOOK! OUR HOMETOWN BATSMAN SMASHED THE BALL, AND IT'S COMING THIS WAY!

GET YOUR GLOVE UP, SON!
NO! I HATE THE BIG-FINGER GLOVE!

YAAAY!
ARRR! THAT BE THE CATCH OF THE DAY!

SPRINGFIELD 2
SHELBYVILLE 1
I'M BABE GEHRIG!
YES YOU ARE, SHON! YOU SHERTAINLY ARE!
Isotopes 9
THE END

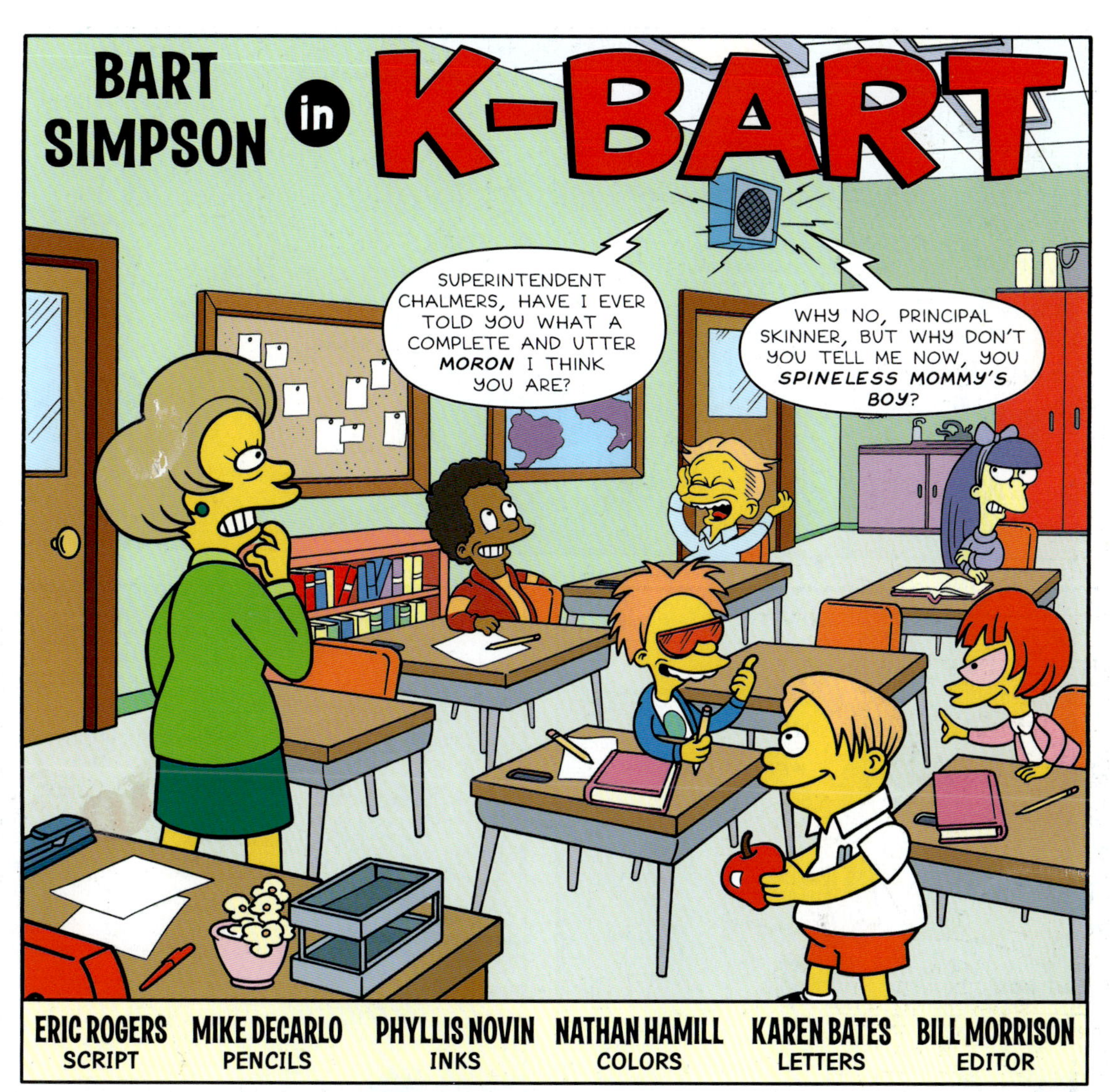

ERIC ROGERS SCRIPT · MIKE DECARLO PENCILS · PHYLLIS NOVIN INKS · NATHAN HAMILL COLORS · KAREN BATES LETTERS · BILL MORRISON EDITOR

NAUGHTY SCHOOL BOARD OFFICIAL! WHAT ARE YOU GOING TO DO TO CHANGE YOUR WAYS?
THWACK!
THWACK!
THWACK!
I'LL SHORTEN THE SCHOOL DAY, ADD ANOTHER RECESS, AND ALLOW THE STUDENTS TO GIVE THE TEACHERS DETENTION!
SKINNER!
I'M RIGHT HERE, AND I HEAR IT, TOO!

YOU KNOW, CHALMY, OL' PAL, I THINK WE SHOULD GIVE THE STUDENTS THE REST OF THE DAY OFF.
HOW 'BOUT THE WHOLE WEEK!
WHO IN BLUE BLAZES IS IMITATING US?!
I DON'T KNOW, BUT THEY'VE REALLY NAILED THAT SLIGHT LISP YOU SOMETIMES LET SLIP...

SKINNER, SHUT UP!
WOO-HOO!
YEAH!
SCHOOL STINKS!

YOU KNOW, I'M GETTING TIRED OF DOING ALL THE PADDLING HERE. WHY DON'T YOU HAVE A GO AT ME NOW, CHALMY?
I THOUGHT YOU'D NEVER ASK!

SO YOU THINK IMITATING SCHOOL OFFICIALS IS FUNNY, DO YOU? WELL, LET'S SEE HOW MUCH LAUGHING YOU DO IN DETENTION FOR THE **NEXT MONTH**!
A MONTH?! YOU CAN'T DO THAT!
YOU JUST WATCH THE SPINELESS MOMMY'S BOY **DO IT**!

YOU REALLY DON'T THINK I'M A SPINELESS MOMMY'S BOY, DO YOU?
SEYMOUR, I TRY TO AVOID THINKING ABOUT YOU **AT ALL**.

WELL, I GUESS WE BOTH KNEW IT WOULD EVENTUALLY COME TO THIS.
WHICH IS WHY I MADE **PREPARATIONS**...

GROSS! YOU'RE EATING SOMEONE'S **OLD GUM**?!?

MY OLD GUM, THANK YOU VERY MUCH. I PUT IT HERE TWO WEEKS AGO FOR JUST THIS KIND OF EMERGENCY.
LOOK, NELSON, YOUR DISGUSTING HABITS ASIDE, I THINK WE WERE PRETTY DARN FUNNY TODAY! WE MAKE A GOOD COMEDY TEAM.

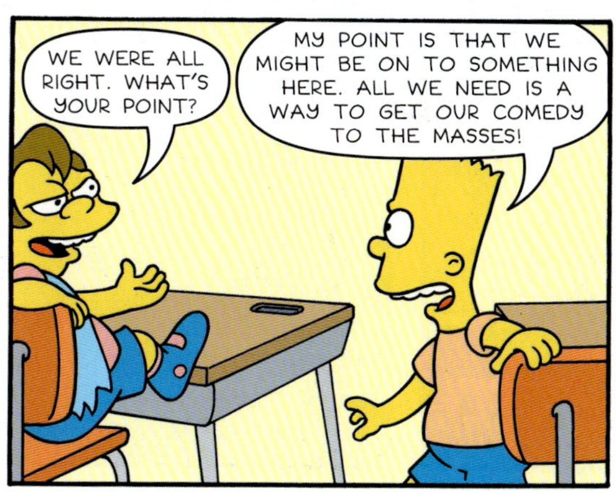
WE WERE ALL RIGHT. WHAT'S YOUR POINT?
MY POINT IS THAT WE MIGHT BE ON TO SOMETHING HERE. ALL WE NEED IS A WAY TO GET OUR COMEDY TO THE MASSES!

LIKE SAY... A RADIO TALK SHOW?
MY MOM ALWAYS SAID I HAD **A FACE FOR RADIO**.

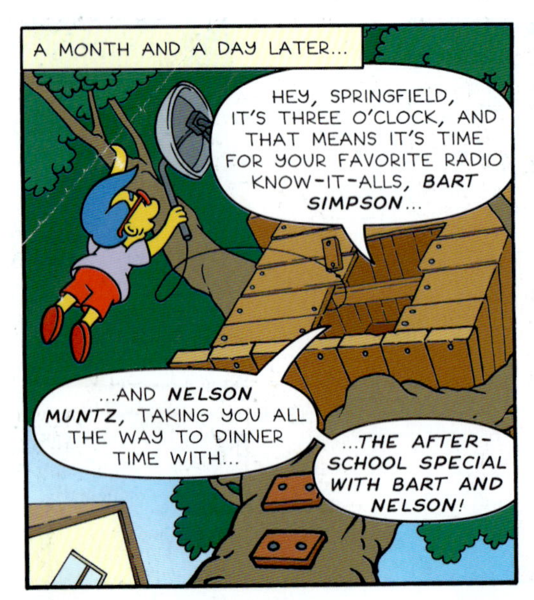
A MONTH AND A DAY LATER...
HEY, SPRINGFIELD, IT'S THREE O'CLOCK, AND THAT MEANS IT'S TIME FOR YOUR FAVORITE RADIO KNOW-IT-ALLS, BART SIMPSON...
...AND NELSON MUNTZ, TAKING YOU ALL THE WAY TO DINNER TIME WITH...
...THE AFTER-SCHOOL SPECIAL WITH BART AND NELSON!

NELSON, MY MAN, HOW WAS SCHOOL TODAY?
A LOT LIKE A KEVIN COSTNER MOVIE... LONG, SERIOUS, AND FULL OF OLD PEOPLE WHO SAY BORING THINGS.

AAA-OOOO-GAH!
WHAT ABOUT YOUR DAY, BART?
I'M AFRAID I'M GETTING SICK, NELSON. THE DOCTOR SAYS IT'S FINGERALIS FLATUENTIA. WHAT-EVER YOU DO, DON'T PULL MY FINGER.

YOU MEAN LIKE THIS?
FRRRRRT!
OH THE PAIN, THE PAIN! BWA-HA-HA-HA!

BOYS, HAVE YOU SEEN OUR SATELLITE DISH? IT'S SUDDENLY GONE MISSING...
HA! HA! HA! HA! HA! HA!
GEE, BART, I HOPE YOU FEEL BETTER!

HA! HA! HA! HA! HA! HA! HA! HA!
IF YOU KEEP PULLING MY FINGER, I'M SURE I WILL!
FRRRRRT!

FRRRRRT!
HA! HA! HA! HA!
ANYTHING FOR A FRIEND!

AH, MUCH BETTER! LET'S GO NOW TO OUR GIRL WITH THE LOWDOWN ON YOUR SLOW-DOWN, LISA SIMPSON!
HA! HA! HA! HA! HA! HA! HA!

BART, TRAFFIC IS FLOWING SMOOTHLY WITH NO ACCIDENTS TO SPEAK OF.

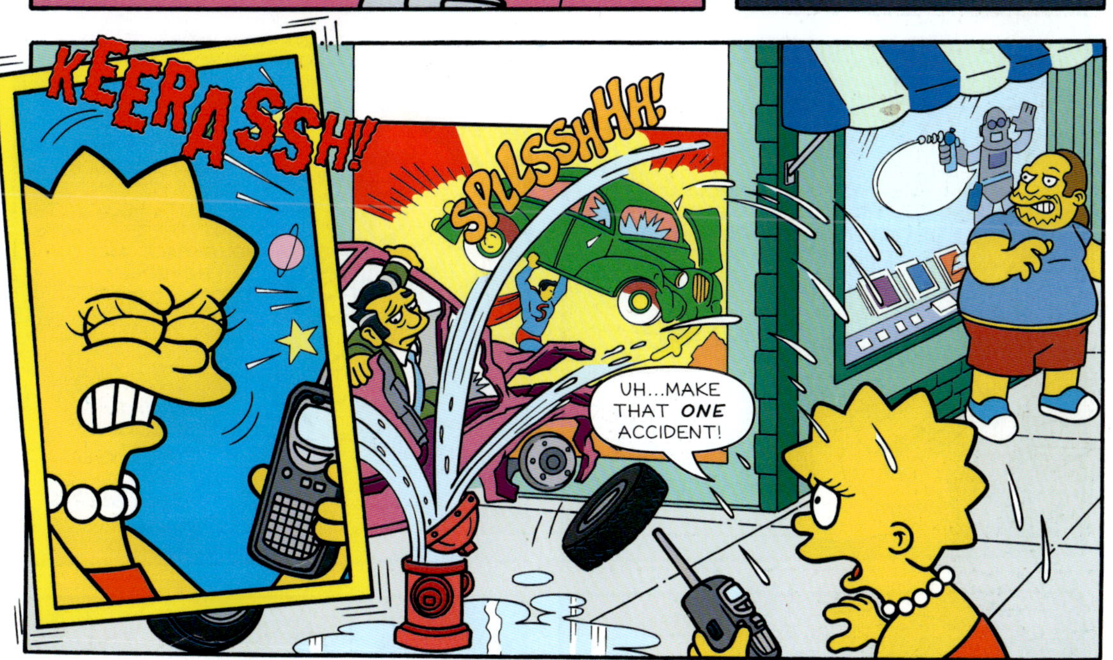
KEERASSSH!!
SPLSSHHH!
UH...MAKE THAT **ONE** ACCIDENT!

LITTLE GIRL, I NEED YOUR HELP!
I NEED TO FIND THE DYNAMIC COMEDY DUO OF BART AND NELSON! DO YOU KNOW WHERE THEY MIGHT BE?
ONCE AGAIN, THE MAN OF STEEL SAVES THE DAY!
I CAN TAKE YOU TO THEM.

BOYS, MY NAME IS FRED POWLUS AND I'M THE STATION MANAGER AT RADIO STATION KBOR, THE 24/7 TALK STATION. I HEARD YOUR SHOW TODAY, AND I THINK IT COULD BE THE NEXT BIG THING!
ARE YOU SAYING YOU WANT OUR SHOW ON YOUR RADIO STATION?!

THAT'S EXACTLY WHAT I'M SAYING, BART! I WANT TO MAKE YOU AND NELSON STARS!
BUT HOW DO WE KNOW HE'S NOT GOING TO COMPROMISE THE INTEGRITY OF OUR WORK? THE ONLY WAY I SAY YES IS IF NO ONE MESSES WITH OUR FORMULA FOR SUCCESS!
WE'RE IN, MAN!

NELSON, IF ANYTHING, I WANT EVEN MORE OF YOUR FORMULA! YOU CAN KEEP DOING THE SHOW HERE IN THE TREEHOUSE, PUSHING THE LIMITS OF WHAT YOU THINK WORKS TO THE ABSOLUTE BRINK! TAKE FOR INSTANCE, THE BOY WHO HANDLES YOUR SATELLITE FEED IN THE TREE OUT THERE! THAT'S IN-YOUR-FACE AND ON-THE-EDGE!
CAN'T KEEP MY GRIP...SOMEONE PLEASE HELP...

SO WHAT DO YOU SAY, BOYS? DO WE HAVE A DEAL?
YAAAHHH..
THWWUMP!
LET'S DO IT!
AWESOME!

WHAT A GREAT BIT! YOU TWO ARE COMEDY GENIUSES!
OHHH, THE PAIN... I CAN'T FEEL MY LEGS...
UHHH... YEAH. THAT'S US.

...AND THAT'S WHY THOSE PEOPLE SHOULDN'T BE ALLOWED ON AIRPLANES, AT SPORTING EVENTS, OR AT CHURCH POT-LUCK DINNERS. YOU'RE LISTENING TO BIRCH BARLOW...WE'LL BE RIGHT BACK.

MONTY, WHAT'S WRONG?
WE'RE LOSING LISTENERS TO THAT NEW SHOW OVER ON KBOR, THE ONE WITH THOSE TWO SNOT-NOSED, IT'S-OPEN-SEASON-ON-EVERYONE BRATS!

ARE THESE NUMBERS CORRECT?
AND IT'S ONLY GETTING WORSE! I'M TELLING YOU, BIRCH, THIS AFTERNOON DELIGHT SHOW IS THE TALK OF THE TOWN, AND WE NEED TO DO SOMETHING ABOUT IT!

THEN DO SOMETHING WE WILL, MONTY.

OKAY, KRUSTY, IN ALL SERIOUSNESS...YOU'VE TAKEN A LOT OF PIES IN THE FACE OVER THE YEARS. BETWEEN US, RIGHT HERE AND NOW ON OUR SHOW...WHO GAVE THE BEST PIE?
HEY, HEY! YOU GUYS REALLY **ARE** OUTRAGEOUS!
DON'T BE SHY, WE'RE ALL FRIENDS HERE.

HI, KIDS, HOPE I'M NOT INTERRUPTING. I'M BIRCH BARLOW, AND I'VE COME TO OFFER MY CONGRATULATIONS ON YOUR SUCCESS.
BIRCH BARLOW?! THE ULTRACONSERVATIVE RADIO PERSONALITY?

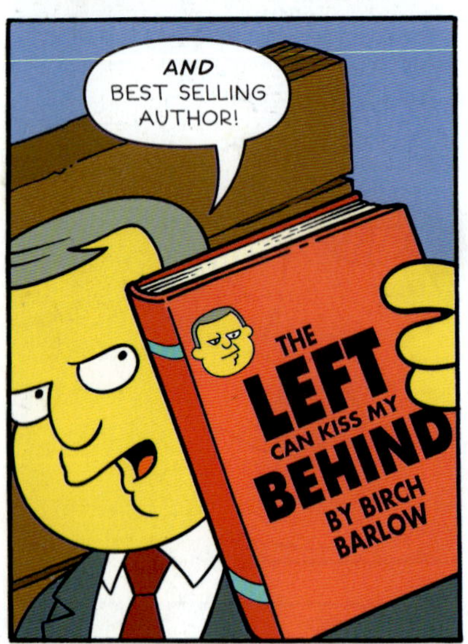
AND BEST SELLING AUTHOR!
THE LEFT CAN KISS MY BEHIND BY BIRCH BARLOW

BOYS, I'M HERE TO MAKE YOU AN HISTORIC DEAL. I KNOW A GOOD THING WHEN I HEAR IT, AND, FRANKLY, YOUR SHOW'S THUMPING MINE IN THE RATINGS **BUT GOOD!**
SO HOW WOULD YOU LIKE TO BROADEN YOUR AUDIENCE **TEN-FOLD** AND RECEIVE A HUNDRED DOLLARS A WEEK **EACH**?
HOW CAN WE DO **THAT**?

BY SIMPLY SIGNING THIS CONTRACT WHICH WILL GIVE RADIO STATION **KSUK**, HOME OF **MY** SHOW, THE **EXCLUSIVE RIGHTS** TO BROADCAST YOUR SHOW.
WE'LL MOVE YOU INTO ONE OF OUR SPIFFY STUDIOS WHERE YOUR SHOW WILL AIR AFTER MINE EVERY DAY FROM SEVEN TO MIDNIGHT!

BUT WE LIKE DOING THE SHOW HERE IN THE TREEHOUSE.
AND I CAN'T DO IT AFTER SEVEN. THAT'S WHEN I DO MY BEST **HOOLIGANNING** AND **NO-GOOD-NIKKING!**

DID I MENTION I'LL ALSO GIVE YOU EACH A DVD COPY OF THE COMPLETE FIRST SEASON OF "THE ITCHY AND SCRATCHY SHOW"?
MMMM... COMPLETE FIRST SEASON...
SIMPSON, GET A HOLD OF YOURSELF, DUDE!
ITCHY & SCRATCHY

SIGN THE CONTRACT, OR YOU'LL BE SORRY!
NO WAY! WE'RE NOT SELLING OUT TO ANYONE!
ITCHY & SCRATCHY

SUIT YOURSELF, YOU LITTLE MUSH-BRAINED SQUAWK BOXES. WE'LL SEE WHO'S STANDING WHEN THIS IS ALL OVER.

BIRCH BARLOW CAN'T KEEP US FROM DOING OUR SHOW...CAN HE?
I DON'T KNOW. THAT GUY'S GOT SOME SERIOUSLY POWERFUL FRIENDS.
THE REPUBLICAN PARTY?
THE MOB?
TOUGHER. RUSSELL CROWE!

I'M SURE WE HAVE NOTHING TO WORRY ABOUT.
YEAH. HE'S JUST TRYING TO SCARE US IS ALL.

A FEW DAYS LATER...

...SO THAT'S WHEN I DROPPED MY SHORTS AND--
SKSSZZZEENNZZ!
OW! WHAT'S GOING ON IN OUR HEADPHONES?!
I DON'T KNOW. I THINK WE LOST OUR SIGNAL!

FACING DOWN THE TREE-HUGGING LIBERALS SO YOU DON'T HAVE TO.
BIRCH BARLOW
WEEKDAYS FROM 3 TO 7 ON
KSUK AM
NO FAIR! BARLOW'S BLOCKING OUR SATELLITE FEED!

WHAT DO YOU MEAN YOU'RE CANCELLING YOUR APPEARANCE ON OUR SHOW?
EXACTLY THAT, BOYS. BIRCH BARLOW IS AN OLD FRIEND OF MINE AND A FELLOW STONECUTTER. NOW, IF YOU'D BE SO KIND AS TO START RUNNING...
WHY?

IT'S MORE SPORTING FOR THE HOUNDS!
BZZT!

AHHHHHH!
SMITHERS, THIS REALLY SHOULD BE AN OLYMPIC EVENT.
YES, SIR.

AND A FEW DAYS AFTER THAT...

...AND WITHOUT THAT AD REVENUE, IT'S IMPOSSIBLE TO KEEP THIS SHOW ON THE AIR! I'M SORRY, BOYS.
BIRCH BARLOW IS THE CREEP BEHIND THIS, BUT HOW DO WE STOP HIM?
HE WANTS TO PLAY ROUGH? FINE. I CAN GO WEDGIE-FOR-WEDGIE WITH THE BEST OF 'EM!

NELSON, HOW ARE WE GOING TO WIN AGAINST BARLOW? HE'S ONE OF THE MOST POWERFUL PEOPLE IN TOWN!
HE WASN'T ALWAYS A BIG SHOT, AND I HAVE **PROOF!**

"WHEN WE WERE GETTING THE SHOW READY TO AIR, I DECIDED TO FIND OUT HOW A RADIO STATION OPERATES. SO I INTERNED AT KDRK, THE STUDENT-RUN STATION AT SPRINGFIELD UNIVERSITY."
...THAT WAS "MIRROR IN THE BATHROOM" BY THE ENGLISH BEAT, CLOSING OUT ANOTHER RAD SET ON ***THE NEW WAVE WONDER HOUR!*** WE'LL BE RIGHT BACK AFTER WE PAY SOME BILLS...

WHAT DO ***THESE*** DO?
DON'T ***TOUCH*** ANYTHING! IF YOU WANT TO DO SOMETHING, WHY DON'T YOU GO IN THE BACK AND ORGANIZE THE TAPES OF OLD SHOWS?

"SO THAT'S WHAT I DID."
"THE HAPPENIN' WITH BIRCH-TREE BARLOW AND THE BEAUTIFUL BOHEMIANS"?!

"I TOOK THE TAPES HOME AND LISTENED TO THEM. IT TURNS OUT THEY WERE OF ***BARLOW*** DOING A SHOW WHEN HE WAS IN COLLEGE!"
THIS IS BIRCH-TREE BARLOW WITH MY BEAUTIFUL BOHEMIANS, AND WE'RE HERE TO LET EVERYONE KNOW IT'S COOL TO TAKE OFF YOUR CLOTHES, HUG A TREE, AND TELL ***THE MAN*** WHAT HE CAN DO WITH HIS MATERIAL POSSESSIONS!
GROOVY, BIRCH!
FAR OUT, BIRCH BABY!

HE WAS IN FAVOR OF EVERYTHING HE ***HATES*** TODAY!
WHICH MEANS WE'VE GOT SOME AMMUNITION, DUDE!

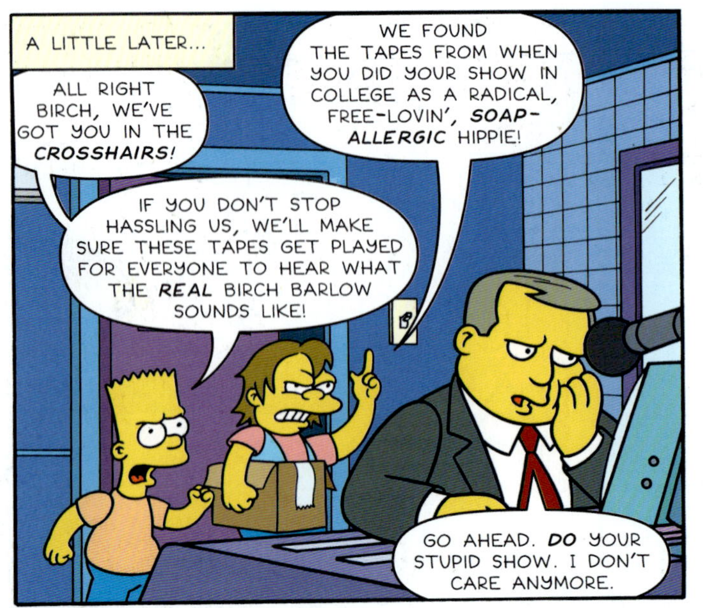
A LITTLE LATER...
ALL RIGHT BIRCH, WE'VE GOT YOU IN THE *CROSSHAIRS!*
WE FOUND THE TAPES FROM WHEN YOU DID YOUR SHOW IN COLLEGE AS A RADICAL, FREE-LOVIN', *SOAP-ALLERGIC* HIPPIE!
IF YOU DON'T STOP HASSLING US, WE'LL MAKE SURE THESE TAPES GET PLAYED FOR EVERYONE TO HEAR WHAT THE *REAL* BIRCH BARLOW SOUNDS LIKE!
GO AHEAD. *DO* YOUR STUPID SHOW. I DON'T CARE ANYMORE.

YOU MEAN YOU'RE NOT GOING TO TRY TO STOP US?
WHAT'S THE POINT? WE'LL ALL BE OUT OF THE TALK RADIO BUSINESS SOON ENOUGH.
WHAT DO YOU MEAN?

HAVEN'T EITHER OF YOU BEEN LISTENING TO THE RADIO THE LAST COUPLE WEEKS? SOMEONE HAS BEAT US AT *BOTH* OUR GAMES!
WHO?!?

JUST LISTEN. IT'S THE NEWEST FAD IN ENTERTAINMENT ...*REALITY RADIO!*
WELCOME BACK TO THE *SPINELESS MOMMY'S BOY DRIVE TIME FUNHOUSE!* NOW, SEYMOUR, TELL US ABOUT THIS NEXT CLIP YOU HAVE FOR US...

DO I REALLY HAVE TO?
IF YOU VALUE *YOUR JOB*, THEN YES!
:SIGH: ALL RIGHT. THIS IS ANOTHER SECRET RECORDING I MADE AT HOME LAST NIGHT AFTER DINNER, WHEN MOTHER ASKED FOR A *SPECIAL FAVOR*...

SEYMOUR!!! GET OFF YOUR KEISTER AND FIND THE BUNYON *FILE!* I'VE GOT A SMALL KNUCKLE GROWING OUT THE SIDE OF MY FOOT, AND YOU'RE GOING TO MAKE LIKE A SUMO WRESTLER AND *FLATTEN* THAT SUCKER!
YES, MOTHER...
BWA-HA-HA-HA-HA!
THE END

Give a Hoot! Read a Book!
HEY-HEY, KIDS!
KRUSTY THE CLOWN SAYS: READ THIS BOOK! HA-HEH!

WHAT?
DID KRUSTY JUST PLUG WHAT I *THINK* KRUSTY JUST PLUGGED?
I *MEAN* IT THIS TIME! YOU ALL BETTER *CAVE* OR YOU'RE *DEAD* TO ME!

CAN WE GO TO THE BOOK-STORE, DAD?
NOT UNTIL YOU FINISH YOUR TELEVISION!
BART! YOU WANT... A BOOK?

LISA, I'M SHOCKED BY YOUR IGNORANCE OF ALL THINGS BART! WHAT IS MY MOTTO?
SIGH "KRUSTY SAID IT, I BELIEVE IT, AND THAT SETTLES IT."
AMEN, SISTER!

HERE, BOY! IF YOU MUST READ, MAKE YOURSELF USEFUL!
I WANT A 25-WORD SUMMARY ON MY DESK IN THE MORNING!
DA-AD!
2005 NUCLEAR SAFETY REGULATIONS

BART'S NEVER SHOWN ANY INTEREST IN BOOKS BEFORE! I THINK YOU SHOULD BUY IT FOR HIM!
YOU DO? THANKS, LIS!

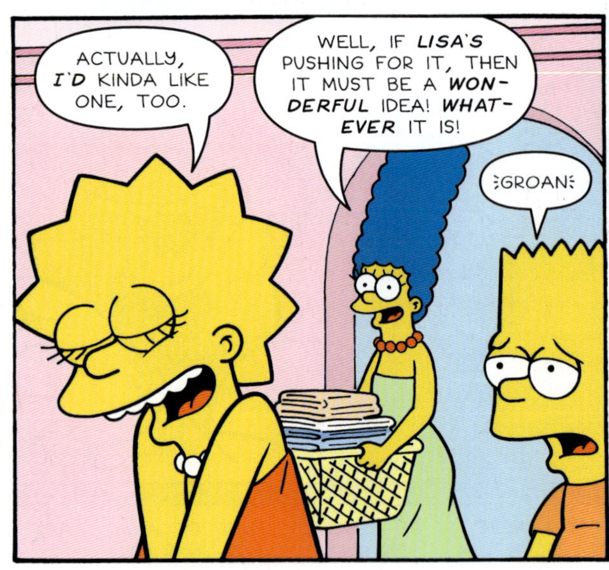
ACTUALLY, I'D KINDA LIKE ONE, TOO.
WELL, IF LISA'S PUSHING FOR IT, THEN IT MUST BE A WONDERFUL IDEA! WHATEVER IT IS!
GROAN

THEN IT'S SETTLED!
WE'VE BEEN TO TANZANIA, JAPAN, BRAZIL, WASHINGTON D.C., NEW YORK, AND CAPITAL CITY! AND NOW...
...THE SIMPSONS ARE GOING TO A BOOKSTORE!
YAAAAY!

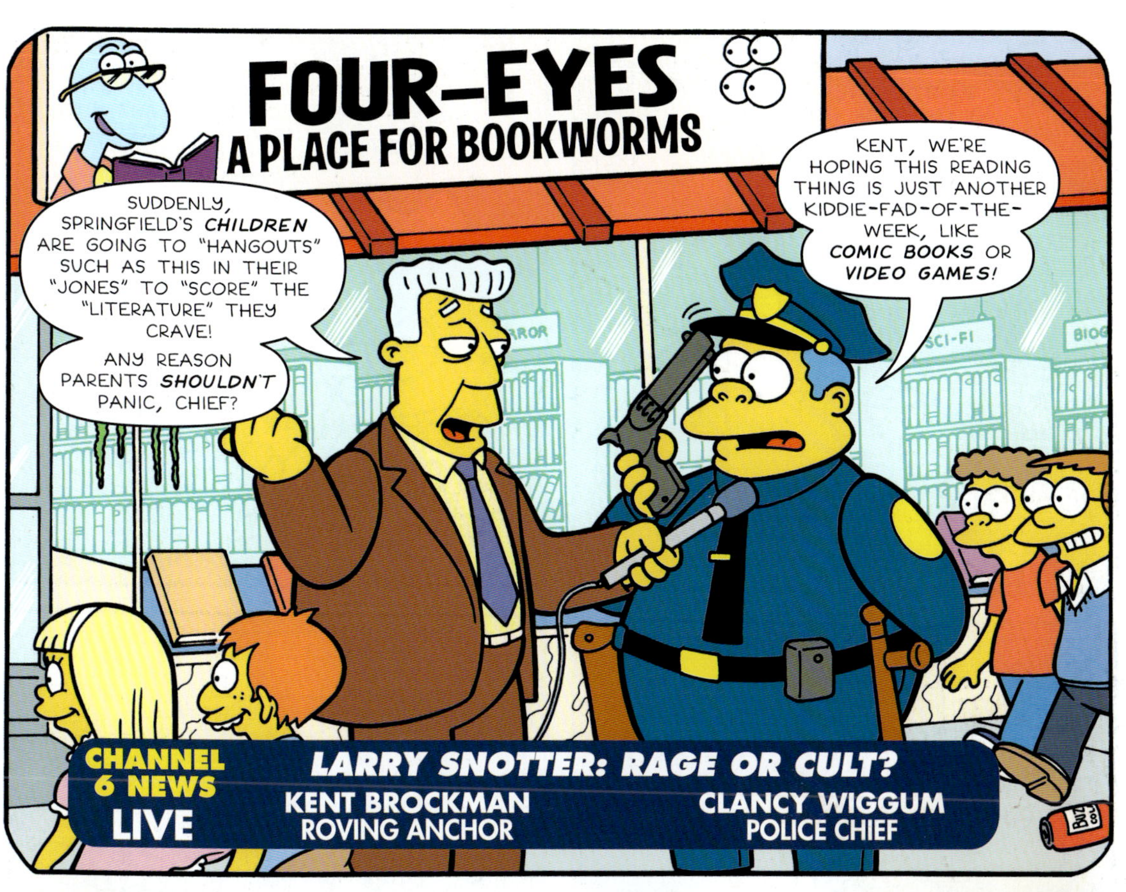
FOUR-EYES
A PLACE FOR BOOKWORMS
SUDDENLY, SPRINGFIELD'S CHILDREN ARE GOING TO "HANGOUTS" SUCH AS THIS IN THEIR "JONES" TO "SCORE" THE "LITERATURE" THEY CRAVE!
ANY REASON PARENTS SHOULDN'T PANIC, CHIEF?
KENT, WE'RE HOPING THIS READING THING IS JUST ANOTHER KIDDIE-FAD-OF-THE-WEEK, LIKE COMIC BOOKS OR VIDEO GAMES!
HORROR
SCI-FI
BIOG
CHANNEL 6 NEWS LIVE
LARRY SNOTTER: RAGE OR CULT?
KENT BROCKMAN ROVING ANCHOR
CLANCY WIGGUM POLICE CHIEF

ISN'T THIS FASCINATING?
YOU PICK OUT ANYTHING YOU WANT AND TAKE IT TO THE CASHIER, JUST LIKE A REGULAR STORE!
CAN I WAIT IN THE CAR?
NO CHECKS

AWW! ONLY ONE COPY LEFT!?
SORRY, LIS, BUT IT HAS TO BE SAID...
LARR SNOT and the sch for monst

YOINK!
LARRY SNOTTER

BART! YOU'VE HAD THE BOOK FOR A LONG TIME! MOM SAID YOU HAVE TO SHARE!
HEH-HEH.

YOU'RE ONLY ON PAGE THREE?
I HAPPEN TO BE SAVORING THE LANGUAGE, LISA! NOW IF YOU EVER WANT YOUR TURN, QUIT SLOWING ME DOWN!

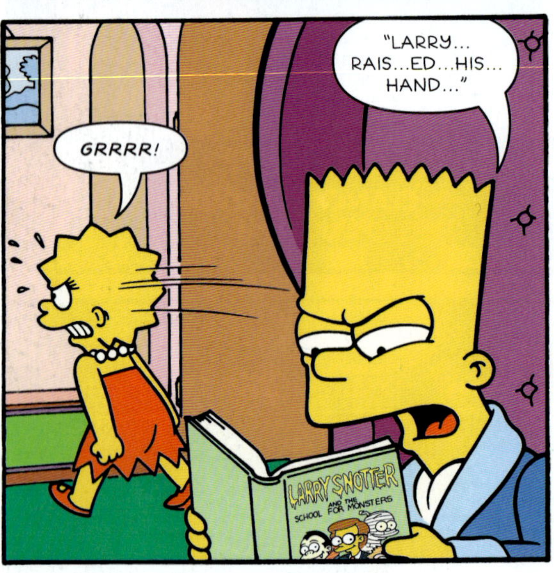
"LARRY... RAIS...ED...HIS... HAND..."
GRRRR!
LARRY SNOTTER AND THE SCHOOL FOR MONSTERS

"...AND ASK...ED...THE TEACH...ER..."
WHAT...IS...THE ...BEST...WAY... TO... SCAR...
SCARE...A KID...THAT'S...BIG... GER...THAN...YOU... ARE...IF...
GRAAA!

GUH!
READING'S WORSE THAN SCHOOL! YOU HAVE TO PAY ATTENTION!
AND FOR SIX HUNDRED MORE PAGES?

NUTS TO THIS!
HAVE FUN IN GEEKVILLE, GEEK!
YAAAY!

GOTTA SHAKE THESE COBWEBS LOOSE!
I'LL HIT THE PLAYGROUND! THERE'S GOTTA BE SOMEBODY THERE TO MESS AROUND WITH...
WHAT THE--?!
LARRY SNOTTER AND THE SCHOOL FOR MONSTERS

HEY, WHO WANTS TO GO **WHIP** THINGS AT SOMETHIN'?
NAAAH! I WANT TO FINISH THIS IN MY LIFETIME, SOMEHOW!
OH, COME **ON**! MY TREAT!

SHUSH!
GO AWAY, BART!
WE'RE BLINKING AT WORDS!
O-KAY...

TAKE IT EASY...
DARE WE BELIEVE OUR **EYES**, EDNA?

CHILDREN USING THEIR **MINDS**? AS IF THEY **WANT** TO?
LORD **HELP** ME, SEYMOUR! I'M ALMOST...**PROUD** OF THEM!

THAT **SETTLES** IT!
THIS ENDS **NOW**!

LATER...
LARRY SNOTTER AND THE SCHOOL FOR MONSTERS

SQUONK!
AAAHH!
WHAT
THE--?

♪ BOOKS! UH-HUH! ♪ UH-HUH! UH-HUH! WHAT ARE THEY GOOOD FOR? ABSOLUTELY NOTHIN'! SING IT AGAIN! ♪ BOOKS--♪

HEY, DOOFUS! KEEP IT DOWN!
JIMBO! KEARNEY! DOLPH!
DON'T TELL ME YOU'RE IN ON THIS!

SO WE'RE LETTIN' OUR IMAGINATIONS TAKE FLIGHT! WHAT'S IT TO YOU?
I JUST GOT TO THE PART WHERE POOR SHOCKZILLA DIED! HE WAS SO BEAUTIFUL!

GROOOOAN
SAY! YOU'RE LOOKIN' KINDA POORLY, BART!

NED FLANDERS!
PLEASED TO SEE ONE PEE-WEE WHO ISN'T PRESSIN' HIS PEEPERS AGAINST THAT PUTRID POTBOILER!

YOU MEAN THE BOOK? YOU AGREE? WITH ME?
OH, WE DON'T GO IN FOR THAT NAST-DIDDLY-ASTY OCCULT STUFF, IF THAT'S WHATCHA MEAN!
SAY, YOU MUST HAVE A PLAYMATE SHORTAGE! WANNA KICK BACK WITH ROD AND TODD?
WE'RE PLAYING "HYMNS!" I'M THE SHEAVES!

YAAAHHHH!

MUST... WATCH...TV!
ALL... I HAVE... LEFT!
KLIK!

...AND WASN'T IT GRIPPING WHEN LARRY SNOTTER CONVINCED ZOMBIE-BOY TO MAKE PEACE WITH HIS FATHER?
I DISAGREE! IT WAS RIVETING, NOT GRIPPING!
KRUSTY'S BOOK CLUB
GAAAH!

I NEVER THOUGHT I'D EVER, EVER SAY THIS...
...BUT KRUSTY MUST BE STOPPED!

...AND I THINK MR. TEENY HAS A POINT ABOUT THE SYMBOLISM IN CHAPTER--
:SIGH!: KEEP IT DOWN!

BAWWWW! FORGET IT! THEY'RE ALL READING!
WHY DO I DO THIS TO MYSELF?
BECAUSE PAROLE BOARDS LIKE BOOKS! OR DO YOU WANT TO WEAR THAT ANKLE BRACELET FOREVER?
PING PING PING

AAAH, JUST FINISH WITHOUT ME! NOBODY'S WATCHING...
...AND I GOT A PENTHOUSE FULL OF LICENSE PLATES THAT AIN'T GONNA STAMP THEMSELVES!

HEY! KRUSTY CAN'T JUST WALK OUT IN THE MIDDLE OF A SHOW! UH, CAN HE, SIR?
HUH? SORRY. WASN'T WATCHING.
EXIT
SLAM!

LOUSY "SESAME STREET!" "OOOH, LET'S TEACH THE CHILDREN TO REEEAD!"
I WARNED 'EM THEY WERE KILLIN' THE GOLDEN GOOSE!

EEEEYAAAAH!
WAAAH!

WHOA! GO EASY, KID! I GOT THIS TICKER ON E-BAY!
I DON'T CARE! ALL MY FRIENDS ARE READING, AND IT'S YOUR FAULT! YOU'VE GOT TO FIX THIS!

LOOK, EVEN IF I TRIED TO GET THAT CRUMMY BOOK BANNED, NOBODY'S WATCHIN' ME ANYWAY!
BANNED? WAIT A MINUTE.
KRUSTY, HOW TIGHT ARE YOU WITH KENT BROCKMAN?

OH, TIGHT. I MEAN, NOT TO SAY HELLO, BUT--
GOOD ENOUGH! LISTEN...

TONIGHT: READING! CAN KIDS HANDLE IT?
AND LATER: WHY THEY CAN'T!
SMARTLINE
I'M KENT BROCKMAN AND THIS IS...SMARTLINE!

NED FLANDERS, TELL US WHY YOU'RE SO WORRIED ABOUT "LARRY SNOTTER."
WELL, KENT, BECAUSE I NEVER READ ANYTHING BUT THE BIBLE! WHO KNOW-DIDDLY-OWS WHAT IDEAS "LARRY SNOTTER" IS CRAMMIN' INTO OUR CHILDRENS' LITTLE NOGGINS?

INDEED. AND HERE TO DEFEND OBSCENITY IS CHANNEL 6'S OWN KRUSTY THE CLOWN.
KRUSTY, NED HAS A POINT! WHY SHOULDN'T WE DESTROY EVERY COPY AND SEND ITS AUTHOR TO SOME BRUTAL FOREIGN PRISON?
FINE, KENT...

...YOU TALKED ME INTO IT!
MARGE! WAKE THE KIDS!
WE'RE GONNA HAVE US A GOOD OLD-FASHIONED BOOK-BANNING!

BAN THE BOOK!
THINK OF THE CHILDREN!
NOW, HONEY, WE'RE JUST EXERCISING OUR RIGHT TO FREEDOM OF SPEECH IN ORDER TO SHUT SOMEONE UP FOREVER!
DAD, THIS IS SCARY! AND UN-AMERICAN!
ATTENTION SPRINGFIELDIANS...

...BY THE POWERS THAT AREN'T REALLY VESTED IN ME...
...I HEREBY BAN ALL "LARRY SNOTTER" BOOKS!
YAAAY!

BURN IN THE PITS OF HELL, LARRY SNOTTER!
AND TAKE YOUR RICHLY IMAGINED WORLD AND STRONG CHARACTER DEVELOPMENT WITH YOU!
NOOOOO!

FWOOOSH!

LATER...
CAN BART COME OUT TO PLAY? I FOUND SOME RUSTY HUBCAPS TO SMASH!
I DOUBT IT. HE NEVER SEEMS TO GO ANYWHERE...

"...SINCE THEY BANNED THAT BOOK!"
"AND... LARRY...SAID... GREEAAAH..."
GIGGLE!
THIS BOOK'S NOT HALF BAD!
THE END

THE SECRET LIFE OF BART SIMPSON

STEP ASIDE, JIMBO!
MCBART! YOU'RE A COP, NOT A TEST PILOT!
IT'S CERTAIN DEATH TO FLY THIS EXPERIMENTAL NANO-PLANE!
STOP

LORD DEATHBOTTOM WILL TRIGGER DER GIRL-GERM BOMB IN 90 SECONDS! DIS PLANE'S MY ONE CHANCE TO STOP IT IN TIME!
MCBART, I'M NOT ASKING, I'M ORDERING YOU--

EAT MY SHORTS!
POW!
STOP

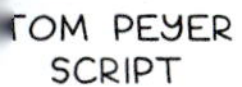

TOM PEYER SCRIPT
JAMES LLOYD PENCILS
ANDREW PEPOY INKS
ART VILLANUEVA COLORS
KAREN BATES LETTERS
BILL MORRISON EDITOR

BEWARE, LORD DEATHBOTTOM...
SKREEEE

...MCBART IS COMING FOR YOU!
SKREEEE
AH! DERE IS HIS RATS' NEST NOW!

RATS' NEST! EVERYBODY OFF!
HUH?
BART! YOU WERE DAYDREAMING AGAIN, WEREN'T YOU?

IT'S ALL YOU'VE BEEN DOING FOR DAYS! I KNOW SCHOOL CAN BE BORING AND HUMILIATING...
...BUT IF YOU DON'T FACE REALITY, YOU'LL NEVER SUCCEED! IS THAT WHAT YOU WANT?
WELL... IS IT?
STOP

YOU ARE A RING BEARER, FRODO! TO BEAR A RING OF POWER IS TO BE ALONE!
GUUHH!

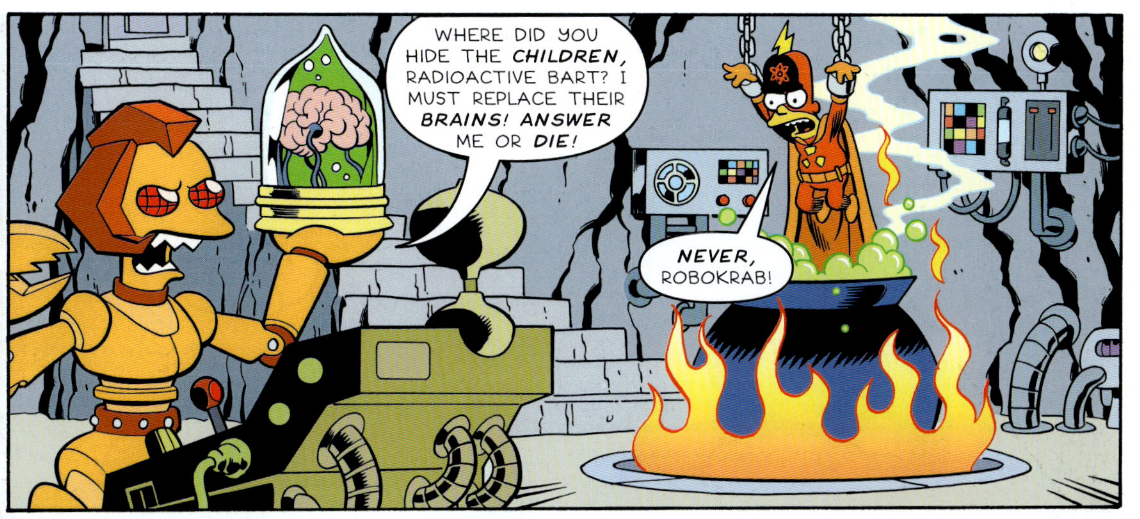
WHERE DID YOU HIDE THE **CHILDREN,** RADIOACTIVE BART? I MUST REPLACE THEIR **BRAINS! ANSWER** ME OR **DIE!**
NEVER, ROBOKRAB!

BART, USE YOUR **BRAIN!** WHAT'S 2 X 4? **ANSWER** ME!
NEVER, YOU **MONSTER!**

UHHH... PRINCIPAL'S OFFICE?
OH YEAH.

SKINNER!
GAAAAH!

SUPERINTENDENT SIMPSON!
I FEEL LIKE FIRING SOMEONE TODAY! GIVE ME 50 REASONS IN 60 SECONDS WHY IT SHOULDN'T BE YOU!
GUHH-UHH-UHH--

SIMPSON!
SIMPSON!
WHERE'S YOUNG SIMPSON?
HUH--?!

I TRIED TO CARRY HIM OUT, BUT HE WAS DEAD WEIGHT!
HE MUST HAVE BEEN DAYDREAMING! HOW SAD! OH WELL...

...ALL THE MORE ICE CREAM AND KITTIES FOR THE KIDS WHO SURVIVED THE FIRE!
YAAAY, BART!
BART! BART! BART!

BART! ARE YOU DAYDREAMING?
I WARNED YOU ABOUT USING YOUR IMAGINATION!
GAAAH!

DON'T WORRY, SEYMOUR!
I'M NEVER TOUCHIN' THAT STUFF AGAIN!
THE END

THE GREAT TRAIN WRECK

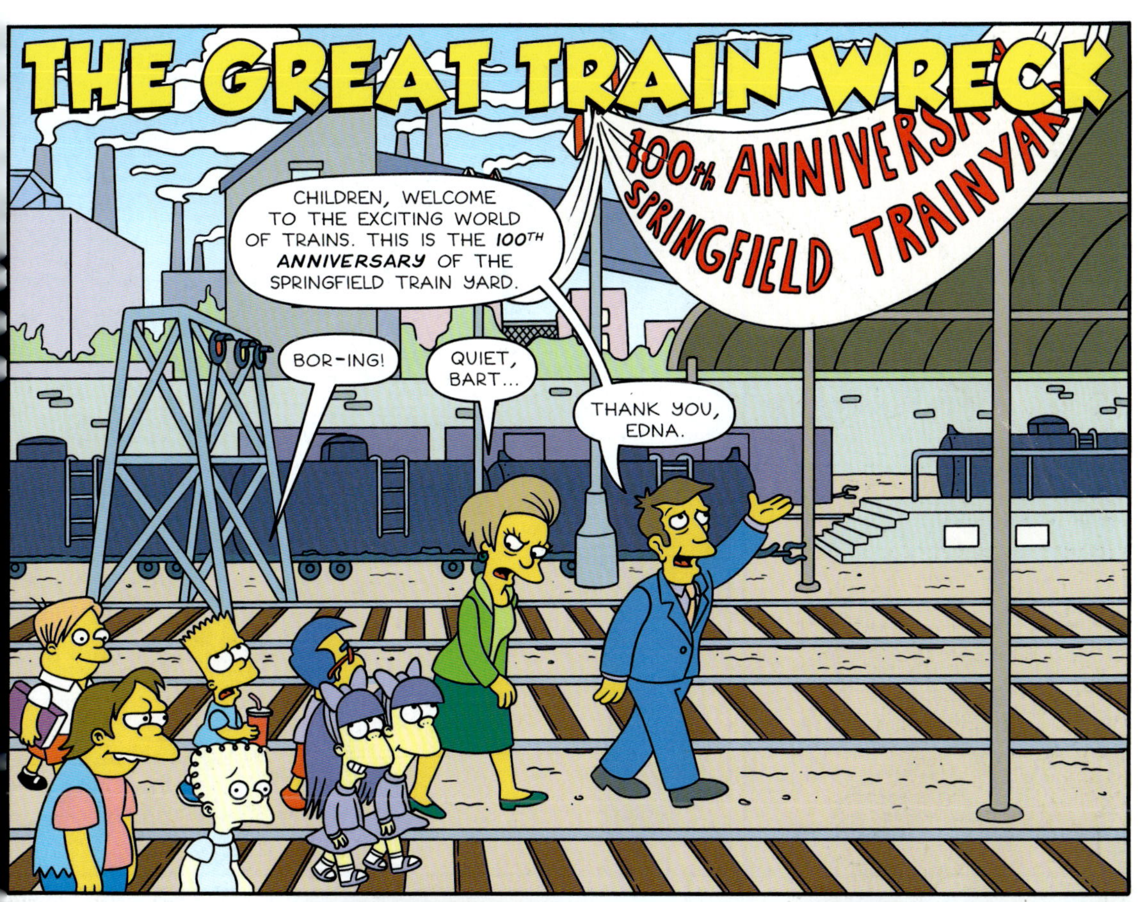

100th ANNIVERSARY SPRINGFIELD TRAINYARD
CHILDREN, WELCOME TO THE EXCITING WORLD OF TRAINS. THIS IS THE 100TH ANNIVERSARY OF THE SPRINGFIELD TRAIN YARD.
BOR-ING!
QUIET, BART...
THANK YOU, EDNA.

...WE'RE ALL BORED OUT OF OUR MINDS! YOU DON'T HAVE TO KEEP REMINDING US!
UH...YES...QUITE. MOVING ON. THE TRAIN YARD, IN HONOR OF THE ANNIVERSARY, HAS DECIDED TO BRING OUT OF RETIREMENT SPRINGFIELD'S VERY FIRST LOCOMOTIVE...

...OLD STEAMY!
OLD STEAMY
HEY, KIDS!

TONY DIGEROLAMO SCRIPT
RYAN RIVETTE PENCILS
MIKE ROTE INKS
ART VILLANUEVA COLORS
KAREN BATES LETTERS
BILL MORRISON EDITOR

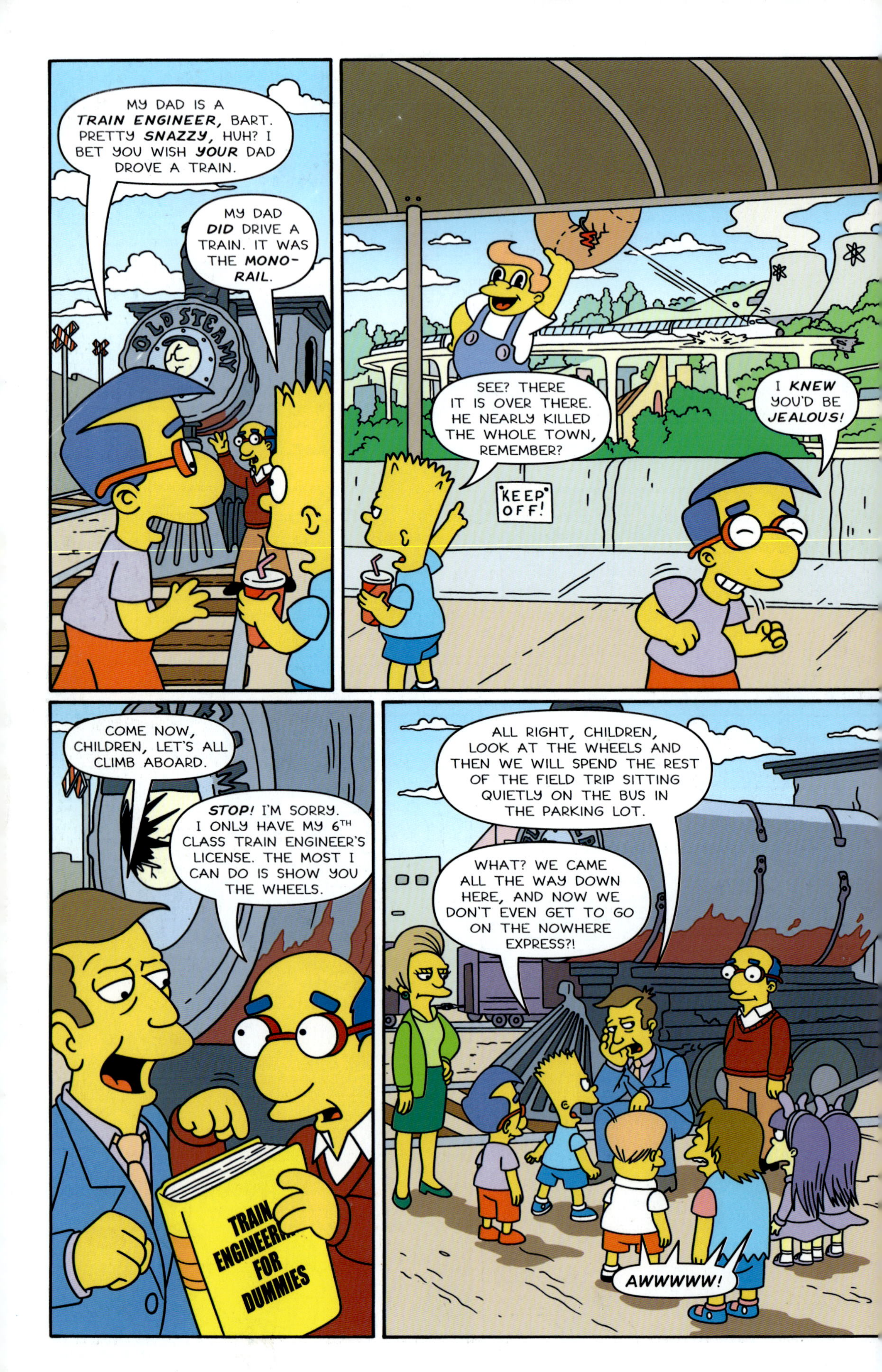
MY DAD IS A TRAIN ENGINEER, BART. PRETTY SNAZZY, HUH? I BET YOU WISH YOUR DAD DROVE A TRAIN.
MY DAD DID DRIVE A TRAIN. IT WAS THE MONO-RAIL.
OLD STEAMY
SEE? THERE IT IS OVER THERE. HE NEARLY KILLED THE WHOLE TOWN, REMEMBER?
KEEP OFF!
I KNEW YOU'D BE JEALOUS!
COME NOW, CHILDREN, LET'S ALL CLIMB ABOARD.
STOP! I'M SORRY. I ONLY HAVE MY 6TH CLASS TRAIN ENGINEER'S LICENSE. THE MOST I CAN DO IS SHOW YOU THE WHEELS.
TRAIN ENGINEERING FOR DUMMIES
ALL RIGHT, CHILDREN, LOOK AT THE WHEELS AND THEN WE WILL SPEND THE REST OF THE FIELD TRIP SITTING QUIETLY ON THE BUS IN THE PARKING LOT.
WHAT? WE CAME ALL THE WAY DOWN HERE, AND NOW WE DON'T EVEN GET TO GO ON THE NOWHERE EXPRESS?!
AWWWWW!

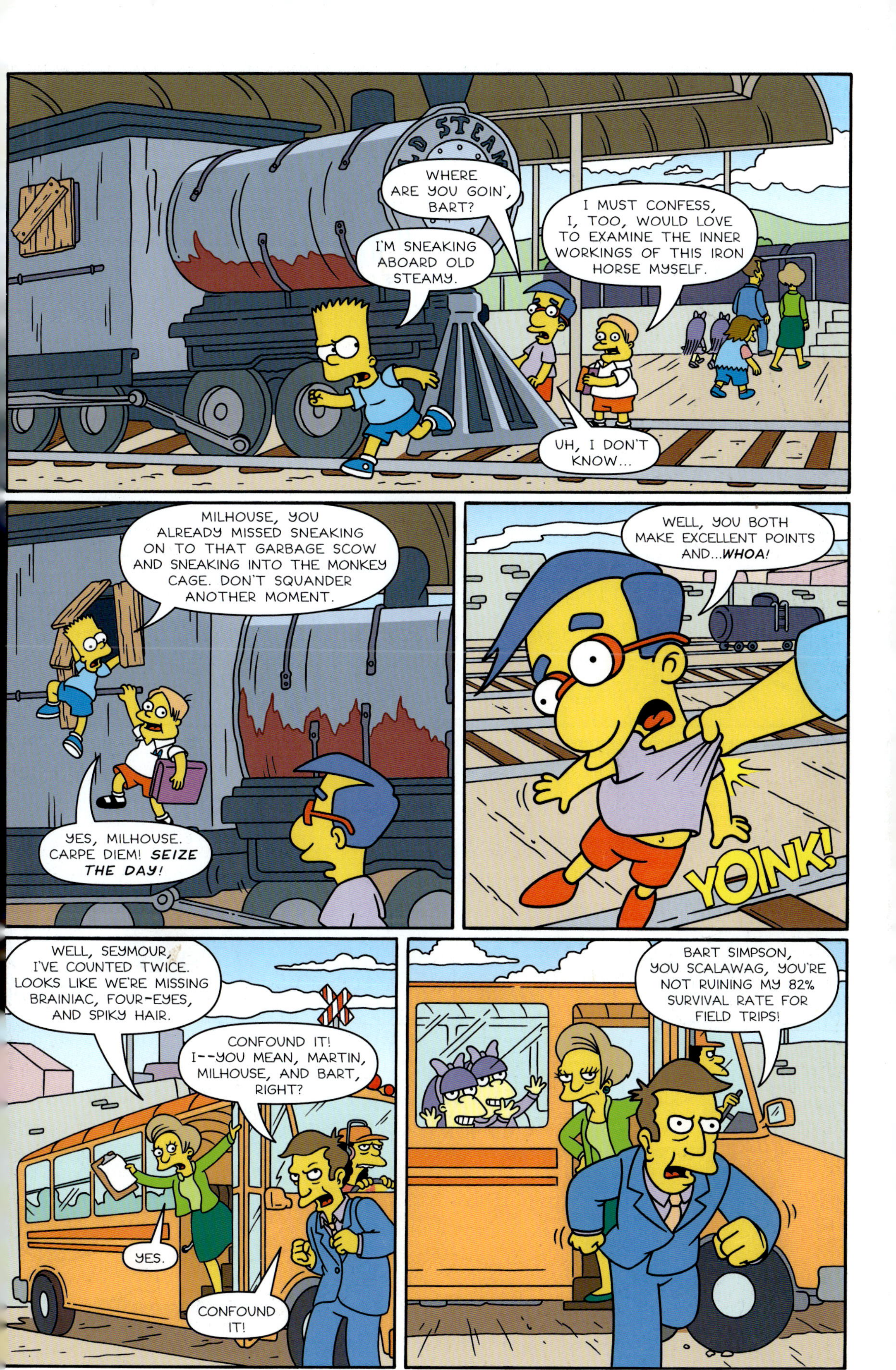
WHERE ARE YOU GOIN', BART?
I'M SNEAKING ABOARD OLD STEAMY.
UH, I DON'T KNOW...
I MUST CONFESS, I, TOO, WOULD LOVE TO EXAMINE THE INNER WORKINGS OF THIS IRON HORSE MYSELF.
MILHOUSE, YOU ALREADY MISSED SNEAKING ON TO THAT GARBAGE SCOW AND SNEAKING INTO THE MONKEY CAGE. DON'T SQUANDER ANOTHER MOMENT.
YES, MILHOUSE. CARPE DIEM! SEIZE THE DAY!
WELL, YOU BOTH MAKE EXCELLENT POINTS AND...WHOA!
YOINK!
WELL, SEYMOUR, I'VE COUNTED TWICE. LOOKS LIKE WE'RE MISSING BRAINIAC, FOUR-EYES, AND SPIKY HAIR.
CONFOUND IT! I--YOU MEAN, MARTIN, MILHOUSE, AND BART, RIGHT?
YES.
CONFOUND IT!
BART SIMPSON, YOU SCALAWAG, YOU'RE NOT RUINING MY 82% SURVIVAL RATE FOR FIELD TRIPS!

WOW! I CAN'T BELIEVE WE'RE ACTUALLY IN THE ENGINE CAB OF A STEAM LOCOMOTIVE!
YEAH, IT'S A REAL THRILL.
WHY DO YOU THINK THEY HAVE SO MANY EXTRA HATS?
I DUNNO. MAYBE THEY HAVE TO CHANGE 'EM A LOT...

...LIKE YOU HAVE TO CHANGE YOUR TRAINING PANTS.
HEY! I HAVEN'T WORN TRAINING PANTS FOR WEEKS! AND YOU **PROMISED** YOU WOULDN'T TELL!
I SAY A LOT OF THINGS.

OH, YEAH! WELL, MAYBE I'LL TELL REVEREND LOVEJOY IT WAS YOU WHO PUT HAIR REMOVER IN THE BAPTISMAL WATER!
WHAT?! YOU **SNITCH**! YOU LAUGHED AT THE BALD BABIES, TOO!
GENTLEMEN! I DON'T THINK WE SHOULD BE SO COMBATIVE IN THE VITAL NERVE CENTER OF THIS POWERFUL METAL BEHEMOTH.

SNAP!
QUIT IT, BART!
YOU QUIT IT!
OH, DEAR! THE START LEVER!

LISTEN, ALL I'M TRYING TO DO IS FIND SOME LOST STUDENTS.
AND I KEEP TELLING YOU, MY 6TH CLASS LICENSE DOESN'T ALLOW ME TO HELP!
WELL, CAN YOU AT LEAST CHECK THE TRAIN?
CH-CHUG
TRAIN ENGINEERING FOR DUMMIES

IN FOUR TO SIX WEEKS, I'LL BE ALLOWED TO LOOK INSIDE THE TRAIN AT TEN MINUTE INTERVALS.
GOOD LORD! THE TRAIN'S MOVING! AND THOSE CHILDREN ARE ON BOARD!
UGGA

CHUGGACHUGGACHUGGACHUGGA
STAY CALM, CHILDREN! I'LL SAVE YOU!
W-WAIT! I'M NOT SUPPOSED TO HAVE ONBOARD GUESTS FOR AT LEAST A YEAR!
TRAIN ENGINEERING FOR DUMMIES

LOOK, CHUMS, WHY BEAT EACH OTHER UP? WE HAVE BULLIES TO DO THAT!
YOU TWO SHOULDN'T LET A COUPLE OF OFF-THE-CUFF REMARKS RUIN YOUR FRIENDSHIP. WE ALL HAVE SECRETS.
HE'S RIGHT, BART. I'M SORRY.
YEAH, I'M SORRY, TOO. BETTER STOP THE TRAIN, MARTIN.

UH...NOW IT'S TIME TO TELL YOU MY DARK REVELATION. THIS SWITCH WAS THE ONLY THING THAT COULD STOP THE TRAIN.
AHHHHHH!

CHUGGACHUGGACHUGGACHUGGA
THERE! NOW TO STOP THIS TRAIN AND THIS TOMFOOLERY!

MOMENTS LATER...
SO THERE'S NO WAY TO STOP THE TRAIN?
I'M AFRAID NOT, PRINCIPAL SKINNER.
THE HISTORY OF TRAINS

AND, ACCORDING TO THE MAP OF THE RAILROAD IN THIS BOOK, THE TRACK FOR OLD STEAMY WAS NEVER FINISHED! THE TRACKS END AT SPRINGFIELD GORGE!
SPRINGFIELD GORGE

WE'RE GOING TO FALL INTO SPRINGFIELD GORGE, BART. BET YOUR DAD'S NEVER DONE THAT!
SURE HE DID. HE WAS IN THE HOSPITAL FOR WEEKS. YOU CALLED THE AMBULANCE, REMEMBER?
I KNEW YOU'D BE JEALOUS!
THE HISTORY OF TRAINS

NO ONE'S FALLING INTO THE GORGE. I'M GOING TO CALL THE POLICE, AND THEY'LL SAVE US.
NO OFFENSE, SEYMOUR, BUT THE COPS IN THIS TOWN COULDN'T CATCH THE MEASLES.

THESE ARE EMERGENCY PROFESSIONALS, BARTHOLOMEW. THEY'LL KNOW WHAT TO DO.
MAP OF SPRINGFIELD
RING! RING!
UH-OH. YA SEE, GUYS, I TOLD YOU THIS WAS GOING TO HAPPEN.

HI, YOU'VE REACHED THE SPRINGFIELD POLICE DEPARTMENT...
WELL, I WANTED TO PLAY CHARADES, CHIEF.
NOT NOW, LOU.

I'M AFRAID WE MAY BE IN TROUBLE, CHILDREN.
C'MON, MARTIN, USE YOUR NERD POWERS.
I'M READING AS FAST AS I CAN! BUT THE HISTORY OF TRAINS SPANS OVER 100 YEARS!

JUST SKIP TO THE PART ABOUT US!
PANICKING ISN'T GOING TO HELP, BART.
WHY, MILHOUSE...HOW CAN YOU REMAIN SO CALM?
THE HISTORY OF TRAINS

I'M NOT WORRIED. WHEN THE TRAIN HITS THAT STALLED TANKER TRUCK WE SHOULD STOP.
MILHOUSE, THAT TRUCK IS CARRYING FUEL. WE'RE GOING TO **BLOW UP!**
GAS

WELL, BART. THIS LOOKS LIKE THE END.
YEAH, MAKES ME FEEL KIND OF **BAD** FOR ALL THE STUFF I DID TO YOU OVER THE YEARS. I'M SORRY I PUT THAT STINK BOMB IN YOUR CAR.
AND I'M SORRY I WROTE ALL THOSE EXPLETIVES IN YOUR PERMANENT RECORD.

I'M SORRY I SWITCHED THE TEACHERS' CHALK WITH CHEESE STICKS.
I'M SORRY I MADE LUNCHLADY DORIS SNEAK BEETS INTO EVERY SINGLE SCHOOL LUNCH YOU ATE.
I'M SORRY ABOUT THE TARANTULAS IN THE TEACHER'S BATHROOM!
I'M SORRY ABOUT MANDATORY MONDAY FILM STRIPS!

AAAAAAAAAH!

THAT THERE FANCY RAILCAR DONE JUST PLUM *TUCKERED OUT!*
HISSSSSSSS

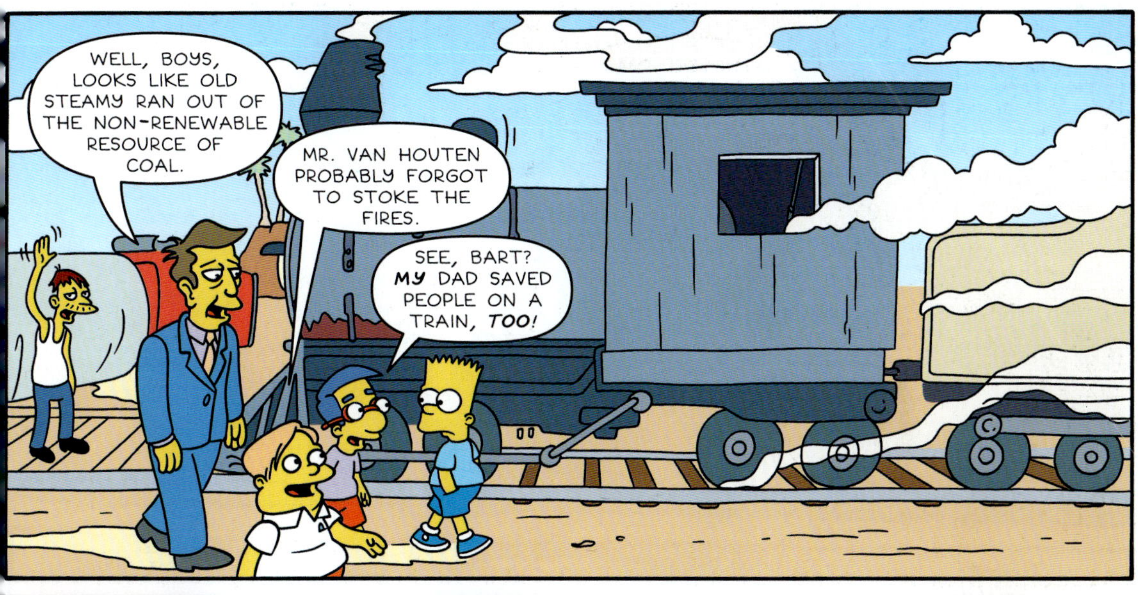

WELL, BOYS, LOOKS LIKE OLD STEAMY RAN OUT OF THE NON-RENEWABLE RESOURCE OF COAL.
MR. VAN HOUTEN PROBABLY FORGOT TO STOKE THE FIRES.
SEE, BART? **MY** DAD SAVED PEOPLE ON A TRAIN, ***TOO!***

LOOKS LIKE WE DIDN'T NEED TO CONFESS ALL THAT STUFF ON THE TRAIN...
UH... YEAH.
BUT AS LONG AS YOU DID, I'M GIVING YOU ***TWO WEEKS DETENTION***.

WHAT?!
BUT WHAT ABOUT ALL THE STUFF ***YOU*** SAID?!
LET THIS BE A LESSON TO YOU, YOUNG MAN. EVEN WHEN FACED WITH THE END, ***NEVER ADMIT TO ANY-THING***.
OH, DON'T WORRY...I'LL BE SERVING DETENTION ***WITH*** YOU.

WAIT A MINUTE. THIS ISN'T RIGHT. USUALLY, BART GETS SKINNER'S GOAT! SKINNER'S NOT SUPPOSED TO ***WIN!*** SKINNER ***NEVER*** WINS!

LATER THAT WEEK IN DETENTION, BART TRICKED SKINNER INTO LOCKING HIMSELF IN A CLOSET, THEN WENT HOME AND WATCHED GIANT APE MOVIES WITH HOMER.

KIRK VAN HOUTEN LOST HIS 6TH CLASS TRAIN ENGINEER LICENSE, AND CHIEF WIGGUM NEVER PLAYED TWISTER AGAIN.

THE END

TONY DIGEROLAMO
SCRIPT

JASON HO
PENCILS & INKS

NATHAN HAMILL
COLORS

KAREN BATES
LETTERS

BART SIMPSON in
SPREE FOR ALL
HEY KIDS! ENTER KRUSTY'S LAND OF MISFIT TOYS GRAND OPENING CONTEST!
ONE LUCKY WINNER WILL GET TO RUN THROUGH THE STORE LIKE A CRAZED GIBBON FOR 5 MINUTES. WHATEVER YOU CAN FIT IN A SHOPPING CART --YOU CAN KEEP!
LOOK! THEY'RE HAVING A SHOPPING SPREE CONTEST!
ONLY ONE ENTRY PER PERSON.
WHOA, MOMMA! FIVE WHOLE MINUTES TO RUN THE GREED GAUNTLET?
LET ME AT THEM ENTRY BLANKS!
EVAN DORKIN SCRIPT
JAMES LLOYD PENCILS
ANDREW PEPOY INKS
NATHAN HAMILL COLORS
KAREN BATES LETTERS
BILL MORRISON EDITOR

HEY, BART! THE RULES SAY ONLY ONE ENTRY PER PERSON!
OW! NOT SO HARD! I HAVE SENSITIVE DORSAL FLESH!
YEAH, RIGHT. THAT'S JUST TO SCARE OFF THE SUCKERS. WHO'S GONNA EVEN NOTICE?
SCRIBBLE
SCRIBBLE
SCRATCH

SORRY, CHIEF, IT'S ONE ENTRY PER PERSON, NO MATTER HOW BIGGIE-SIZED THAT PERSON MAY BE.
WHY, YOU-- THIS IS AN OUTRAGE! I DEMAND A CHALLENGE RITUAL BEFORE A FULL KLINGON COUNCIL!
LUCASFILM IS MY CO-PILOT

HEY K... LAND ... GRAND OPENIN...
ON SECOND THOUGHT, I'LL JUST PUT IN ONE ENTRY. YOU KNOW, SPIRIT OF FAIR PLAY AND ALL THAT CRUD.

BOOK NOOK
THRIF...
IF I WIN, THE FIRST THING I'LL GET IS THE RADIOACTIVE MAN VIDEO GAME THE SENATE IS TRYING TO BAN BECAUSE OF ADULT CONTENT.
THE FIRST THING I'LL DO IS REGURGITATE FROM SHEER EXCITEMENT! THEN I'D GRAB A STUFFED ANIMAL SIBLING SUBSTITUTE TO HUG DURING MY LONELIER MOMENTS.

DARE TO DREAM, DUDES. MAYBE I'LL GRAB THAT JUNK FOR YOU ON MY WAY TO AISLE 12, HOME OF THE NEW KID-TASTIC KRUSTY-BOT WITH 102 DIFFERENT FUNNY FUNCTIONS AND 12 HIDDEN DANGERS!
YEAH, RIGHT. HOW CAN YOU BE SO SURE YOU'LL WIN?
BECAUSE I'M BART SIMPSON, MAN. DON'T YOU GET IT?

...BREAKING REPORT OF WAR WITH NORTH KOREA, BUT FIRST...WE GO LIVE TO KRUSTY'S LAND OF MISFIT TOYS, WHERE THEY'RE ABOUT TO ANNOUNCE THE WINNER OF THE SHOPPING SPREE CONTEST!
HERE WE GO!
GOOD LUCK, KIDS!

HO-HO-KAY, FOLKS! IT'S THE MOMENT WE'VE ALL BEEN WAITING FOR, WHEN WE FIND OUT WHO GETS FIVE MINUTES TO RUN THROUGH KRUSTY'S LITTLE TAX DODGE!
HEH HEH. I MEAN, TOY STORE.
AND THE WINNER IS...

...BART SIMPSON.
I-I WON--?!

SORRY, BOY. NOT EVERYONE CAN BE A WINNER. WHERE'S THE REMOTE, MARGE? I WANNA WATCH HOCKEY...
I WON!!!

WE HAD A DEAL, CLOWN. MY NEPHEW WINS TOYS, AND YOU DON'T FIND OUT HOW MUCH CEMENT IT TAKES TO FILL THEM FLOPPY SHOES OF YOURS.
I KNOW, B-BUT, Y'SEE... HEH HEH... I LEFT THE LITTLE BAMBINO'S ENTRY IN MY OTHER BAGGY PANTS
OUCH!

I WON! I WON! I'M BART SIMPSON! WINNER!
I'M THE LUCKIEST BOY IN THE WORLD! WOO-HOOOO!
WELCOME

THE NEXT MORNING...
I'VE GOT IT ALL WORKED OUT TO THE SECOND! FIRST STOP, KRUSTY-BOT! THEN ACTION FIGURE ALLEY, THE SKATE-BOARD SECTION, OVER TO AISLE 8 FOR AN ANT FARM, SEA MONKEYS, AND A TUB OF STINKY-DOH...
...LEAVING YOURS TRULY A WHOLE SWEET MINUTE TO PILLAGE THE GAME AND ELECTRONICS ZONE BEFORE JETTING BACK TO THE FINISH LINE!
S
P
SPRINGFIELD TIMES
CONSERVATIVES AHEAD IN CANADA

THAT'S NICE, BART, BUT DON'T YOU THINK YOU SHOULD PICK UP A LITTLE SOMETHING FOR YOUR SISTERS?
OH, BART, **WOULD** YOU?

I'D REALLY LIKE A **MY PRETTY EXPENSIVE PONY**. I REALIZE MY RATHER UNHEALTHY DESIRE FOR ONE SAYS A LOT ABOUT PEER PRESSURE AND THE EFFECTS OF CHILDREN'S ADVERTISING, BUT THEY'RE JUST **SOOOO CUTE**!
PFFT! NO WAY, JOSÉ. I'VE GOT NO TIME FOR DILLY-DALLYING IN THE GIRLY AISLE.

HOMER, TALK TO YOUR SON.
HE KNOWS WHAT HE'S DOING, MARGE. HE'S GOT A **MAP!**
HOMER!
GET YOUR SISTER A STUPID HORSE, BART.

AND WHILE YOU'RE AT IT, BOY, HOW'S ABOUT A **DUFFMAN MINI-FRIDGE** FOR YOUR OLD MAN? IT'S THE **MINI-FRIDGE** THAT HOLDS **MAXI-PLEASURE!**

HMMM, I GUESS I COULD SPARE A FEW SECONDS GETTING DUMB STUFF FOR MY FAMILY.
BUT NOBODY ELSE BETTER GET THE IDEA THEY CAN HIT THE **BARTSTER** UP FOR ANY FREEBIES!
SPRINGFIELD ELEMENTARY SCHOOL

BART! BART! YOU JUST GOTTA GET ME THAT RADIOACTIVE MAN GAME!
PLEASE, BART! CAN YOU GET ME A PLUSH RED PANDA?
I WANT THE PARIS HILTON MAKE-UP AND SURGERY STYLING HEAD!
RC MONSTERTRUCK-ASAURUS!
I WANT POVERTY THE FUN BOARD GAME OF WORKING CLASS AMERICA!
THE BLACK PLAGUE PLAY-MOBIL SET!
WANT LIST
ACTION CREEP!
AYE, CARUMBA!
DUDE, I'D TOTALLY DIG OZZY'S MAKE-YOUR-OWN YUMMY GUMMY BITE-A-BAT KIT!

LATER...
JUST ONE TOY! I'LL DO YOUR HOMEWORK!
I'LL GET YOU ON THE FOOTBALL TEAM!
I'LL TAKE YOUR NEXT THREE BULLY BEATINGS!
I'LL CANCEL YOUR NEXT THREE BEATINGS!

LATER STILL...
I'LL PRETEND TO BE YOUR FRIEND.
I'LL PRETEND BETTER.
I'LL HOLD YOUR HAND, ONCE, IN FRONT OF PEOPLE!
Want List

ETC, ETC...
OKAY, DWEEB, NOW HERE'S THE STUFF I WANT FOR MY KID--
WANT LIST
WANT LISTS
WOOD BURNING SET
WANNT LIST:
DROP TOY WANT LIST/ THREATS OFF HERE

A-HEM!
CHEESE IT, IT'S THE MAN!

SO, BART, I UNDERSTAND YOU'VE BEEN HASSLED A BIT BY YOUR FELLOW STUDENTS OVER THAT TOY CONTEST YOU WON.
TWO PINK BELLIES, THREE PURPLE NURPLES, AND MORE WISH LISTS THAN SANTA GETS IN A YEAR.
DROP TOYS WAN LIST/ THREA OFF HERE

YES, WELL, IF YOU NEED ANY HELP DURING THESE TROUBLING TIMES OF EXTREME PEER PRESSURE, YOU CAN ALWAYS COME TO ME.
HMMM. WHAT'LL IT COST ME?

BART, I'M HURT. AS PRINCIPAL, IT'S MY DUTY TO SEE TO A STUDENT'S WELL BEING.

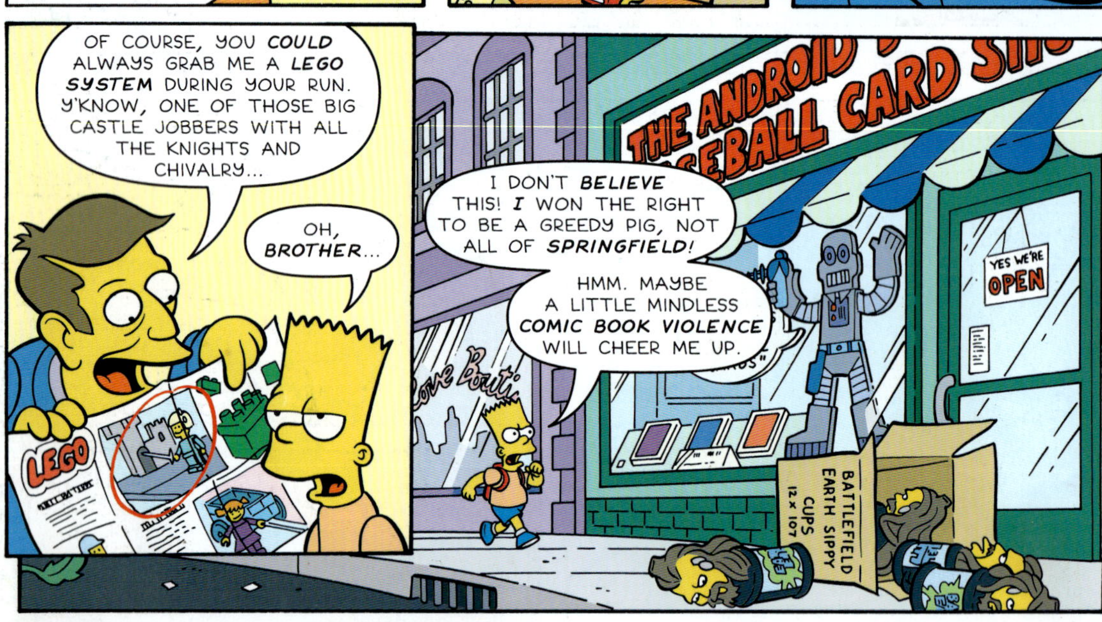
OF COURSE, YOU COULD ALWAYS GRAB ME A LEGO SYSTEM DURING YOUR RUN. Y'KNOW, ONE OF THOSE BIG CASTLE JOBBERS WITH ALL THE KNIGHTS AND CHIVALRY...
OH, BROTHER...
LEGO
THE ANDROID'S
BASEBALL CARD SH
I DON'T BELIEVE THIS! I WON THE RIGHT TO BE A GREEDY PIG, NOT ALL OF SPRINGFIELD!
HMM. MAYBE A LITTLE MINDLESS COMIC BOOK VIOLENCE WILL CHEER ME UP.
YES WE'RE OPEN
BATTLEFIELD EARTH SIPPY CUPS 12 x 107

HALT! NONE SHALL PASS!
HIGHLANDER 2
HUH? WHAT'S THE BIG IDEA, BOUNCING BOY? I'M PAYING IN CASH, NOT IN SHOPLIFTING.

I DON'T CARE IF YOU'RE DOLING OUT DILITHIUM CRYSTALS. YOU, MY LITTLE FRIEND, ARE HEREBY BANNED FOR LIFE... UNLESS YOU AGREE TO STOCK MY LARDER DURING YOUR TOY RUN!
WHICH, I MIGHT ADD, WAS RIGHTFULLY MINE.
McBANE IS BACK!
YOU'RE KIDDING, RIGHT?
HULK FISTS AND FEET
THING FISTS AND FEET
50-CENT FISTS AN AND FEET
ZAGNUT BARS
BOTTLE CAPS
ELEKTRA LIK-A STIK

KA-BOOT!
I GUESS NOT.

:SIGH:
MAYBE WINNING THIS CONTEST WASN'T SO LUCKY AFTER ALL.

AW, MAAAN...
GET ME THESE TOYS OR ELSE!

HEY, BOY, HOW'S MY WINNER? OOH, NICE KNIFE!
SAY, IS THAT ALL YOU GOT? ONE LOUSY KNIFE? YOU COULD'VE GRABBED HUNDREDS OF KNIVES IN FIVE MINUTES!
FUNGUS YUNS
DUFF BEER

I DIDN'T GO ON THE SPREE YET. THE KNIFE WAS IN THE DOOR WITH THIS NOTE THREATENING MY LIFE.
OH, THAT'S DIFFERENT. LOOK, MARGE, FREE KNIFE! IT'S "FREE STUFF WEEK" AT THE SIMPSON HOUSE! WOO-HOO!

ARE YOU ALL RIGHT, BART? YOU LOOK DEPRESSED.
ROUGH DAY, MOM. EVERYONE AND THEIR STEPBROTHER ARE AFTER ME FOR TOYS. THEY'RE TEARING ME APART!

HMMM. I GUESS THIS IS AN AWKWARD TIME TO INTRODUCE YOU TO YOUR LONG-LOST COUSINS FROM THE TINY REPUBLIC OF TOGONIA.
ALLO, BART! LONG TIME NO NEVER SEE! WE BRING YOU GIFT FROM OUR LAND.
SALTED PORK BALLS AND WINT-O-GREEN BANANA GUM! YOU GET US TOYS, YES?
AYE, CARUMBA!

GOOD LUCK IN YOUR MAD DASH FOR GREED, BART. EVEN IF YOU DON'T GET ME ANYTHING, I'LL STILL LOVE YOU BECAUSE YOU'RE MY BROTHER, NO MANY HOW MANY EMOTIONAL SCARS YOU MAY INFLICT ON ME DURING OUR WONDER YEARS.

GOSH, LISA. THANKS!

BART! REMEMBER ME IN MY TIME OF RADIOACTIVE MAN NEED!
DON'T FORGET MY STUFF, SIMPSON! OR YOU CAN FORGET ABOUT YOUR TEETH!
GULP!
PLEASE, BART! I SO NEED COMPANIONSHIP!

WHAT SHOULD I DO? GET WHAT THEY WANT OR GET BEAT UP? LOSE A KRUSTY-BOT OR LOSE MY FRIENDS?
I GOTTA DO WHAT'S RIGHT, AND THAT'S THAT!

HEY, LOSERS! YOU CAN ALL SHOVE YOUR WANT LISTS WHERE THE TP TOILS! BART SIMPSON BOWS TO NO ONE IN THE QUEST FOR PLASTIC TREASURES MADE IN CHINA!
WHATTAYA SAY ABOUT THAT, HUH?!

I SAY WE KICK HIS BUTT!
WHOA, MOMMA! TOTAL RIOTSVILLE!

AISLE 3
HEY, CUT IT OUT! NO PIMPIN' MY RIDE, PLAYER HATERS!
UFF!
PUSH IT TO THE GAMES AISLE!
NO WAY! STEER TO THE ACTION FIGURES!

GET OFF MY HAND!
ALL OF YOU GET OFF! YOU'RE RUINING MY SPREE!
HEY, WATCH IT!
GET OFF MY HEAD!
HEY! HEY!
KRUS
LOOK OUT! WE'RE GONNA HIT THAT--
KRUSTY

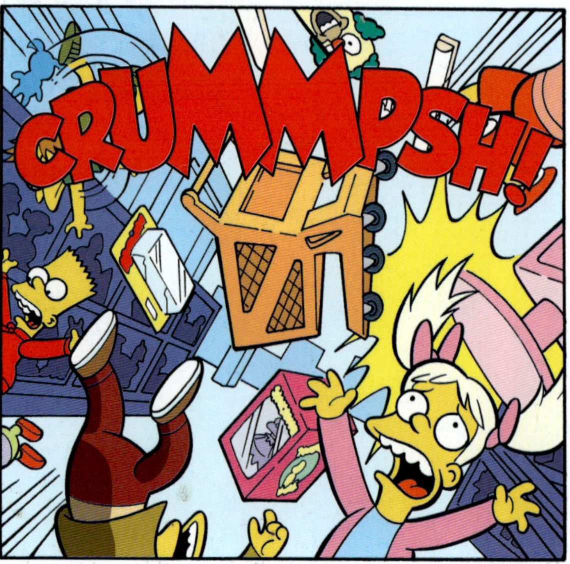

CRUMMPSH!

OH, HOMER, THIS IS TERRIBLE!
TELL ME ABOUT IT! TWENTY BUCKS FOR KEG-HOISTING DUFFMAN?! WHAT A RIP-OFF!

OHHHHHHH... WH-WHERE AM I--?
B-BART! YOU GOTTA GET UP! YOU ONLY HAVE THIRTY SECONDS TO CROSS THE FINISH LINE!

MUST...REACH ...FINISH LINE...SAVE... KRUSTY-BOT...
I'M SORRY, BART! I MUST HAVE BEEN DRIVEN TEMPORARILY INSANE FROM JEALOUSY...OR BREAKFAST.
SORRY I CAN'T HELP, BART. I'M HEMORRHAGING INTERNALLY!

HURRY, BOY! TIME'S ALMOST UP!
MUST... CROSS...FINISH LINE...

SHOP OR I DROP (YOU)
C'MON, BART!
C'MON, BOY! YOU CAN DO IT!
...M-MUST...RETAIN ...KRUSTY-BOT--!

THAT'S IT, BOY! THAT'S IT! YOU-- D'OOOHFF!
TIME'S UP!
BLAMM!

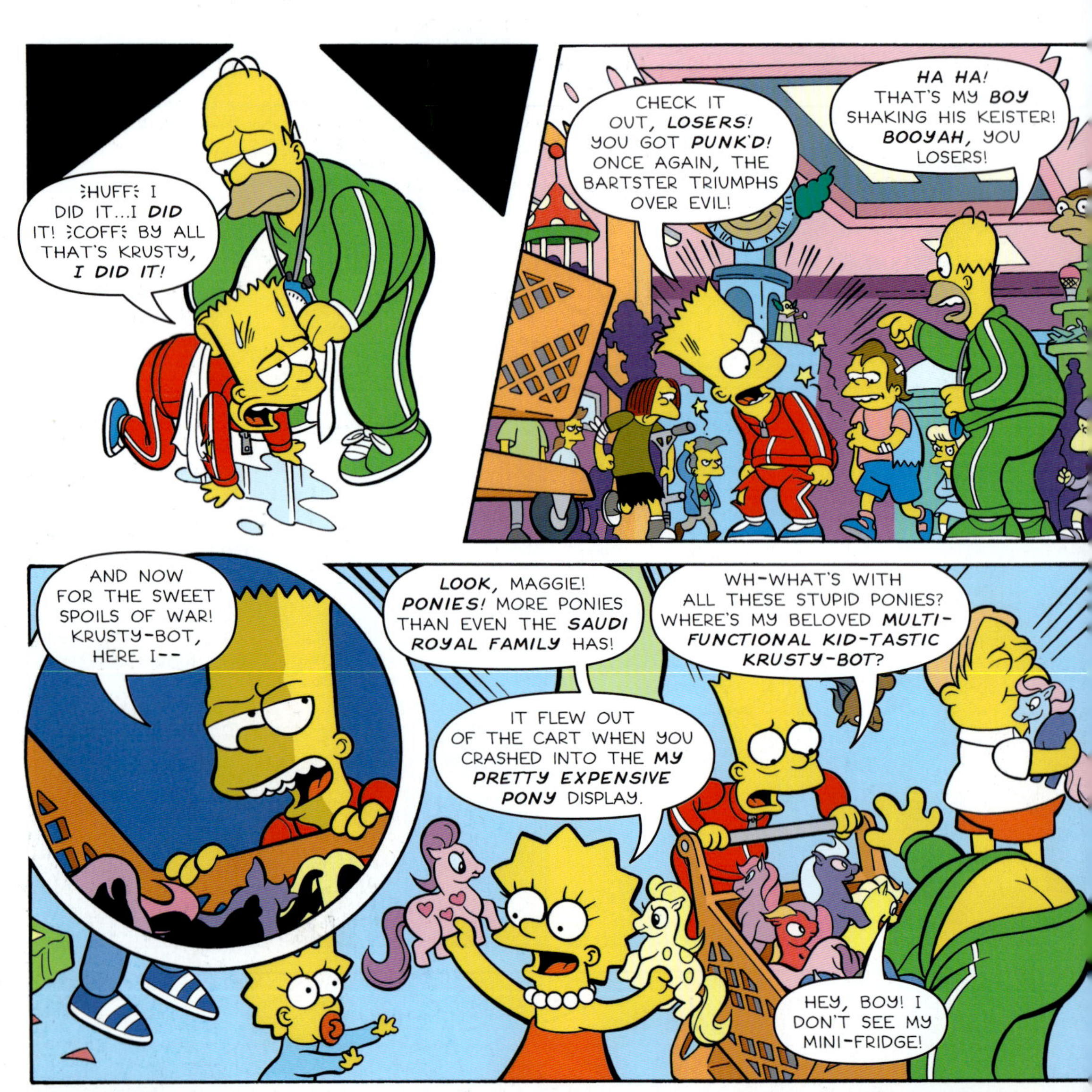
HUFF! I DID IT...I DID IT! COFF! BY ALL THAT'S KRUSTY, I DID IT!
CHECK IT OUT, LOSERS! YOU GOT PUNK'D! ONCE AGAIN, THE BARTSTER TRIUMPHS OVER EVIL!
HA HA! THAT'S MY BOY SHAKING HIS KEISTER! BOOYAH, YOU LOSERS!
AND NOW FOR THE SWEET SPOILS OF WAR! KRUSTY-BOT, HERE I--
LOOK, MAGGIE! PONIES! MORE PONIES THAN EVEN THE SAUDI ROYAL FAMILY HAS!
WH-WHAT'S WITH ALL THESE STUPID PONIES? WHERE'S MY BELOVED MULTI-FUNCTIONAL KID-TASTIC KRUSTY-BOT?
IT FLEW OUT OF THE CART WHEN YOU CRASHED INTO THE MY PRETTY EXPENSIVE PONY DISPLAY.
HEY, BOY! I DON'T SEE MY MINI-FRIDGE!

HA HA! NICE PONIES, SIMPSON!
SEE YOU AFTER SCHOOL, PONY BOY! WE'LL BRING THE PAIN!

WELL, ALL'S WELL THAT ENDS WELL.
EXCUSE ME? MOM, I GOT ROYALLY RIPPED. LISA GOT EVERYTHING, AND ALL MY ENEMIES ARE GONNA TAN MY BUTT AT SCHOOL! HOW CAN YOU SAY THIS ENDED WELL?
WELL... AT LEAST IT ENDED.
THE END

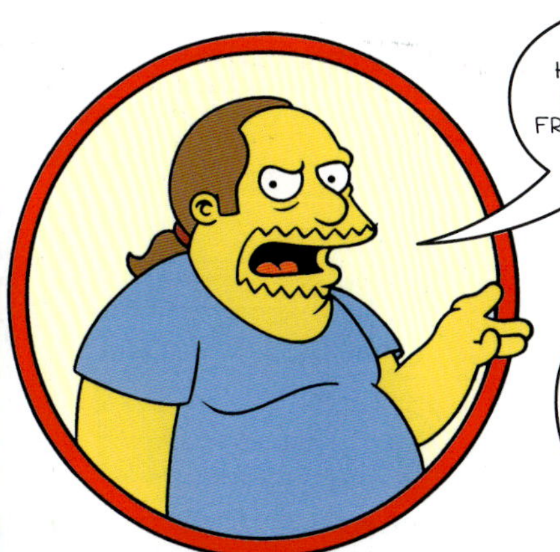

THE TRUE AFICIONADO OF THE POPULAR ARTS WALKS THE WALK, BUT MORE IMPORTANTLY, HE ***TALKS THE TALK!*** PROPER USAGE OF SCIENCE FICTION, HORROR AND FANTASY QUOTES SEPARATES THE ***HE-MEN*** FROM THE ***LOST BOYS***. IF YOU DON'T KNOW "***THE FORCE IS STRONG IN THIS ONE***" FROM "***THROW ME THE WHIP!***" THEN YOU'RE IN THE LATTER CATEGORY, AND YOU NEED HELP! THEREFORE, I SAY "SUBMITTED FOR YOUR APPROVAL" ARE THESE

HANDY POP CULTURE QUOTES FOR ALL OCCASIONS!

STARTING THE DAY
UP AND ATOM!

RADIOACTIVE MAN, ***RADIOACTIVE MAN*** #1-PRESENT

SHOPPING
THE LEFTORIUM
I SEE DEAD PEOPLE.
SALE

COLE SEAR, ***THE SIXTH SENSE***

AVOIDING DISTRACTIONS

DO YOU HAVE BICLOPS #4?
I'M A TRIFLE DEAF IN THIS EAR, SPEAK A LITTLE LOUDER NEXT TIME.

WILLY WONKA, ***WILLY WONKA AND THE CHOCOLATE FACTORY***

APPREHENDING SHOPLIFTERS
YOU'RE UNDER ARREST FOR VIOLATING SECTION 4-1-5-3 OF THE TYCHO TREATY!

AGENT K, ***MEN IN BLACK***

EVAN DORKIN SCRIPT | *JEFF BRENNAN* PENCILS | *MIKE ROTE* INKS | *CHRIS UNGAR* COLORS | *KAREN BATES* LETTERS | *BILL MORRISON* EDITOR

APPRECIATING THE FINER THINGS
I'D BUY *THAT* FOR A DOLLAR!
"TAKE ME TO YOUR COMIC BOOKS & BASEBALL CARDS"
THE "I'D BUY THAT FOR A DOLLAR" GUY, *ROBOCOP*

LOSING GRACEFULLY
NUCLEAR OPTION
THAT'S IT, MAN! GAME OVER, MAN! GAME OVER!
GAME OVER
PRIVATE W. HUDSON, *ALIENS*

ATTENDING TO NATURE
GAMING CONVENTION
KNIGHT'S ROOM
MAIDEN'S ROOM
I'LL BE BACK.
DUNGEON MASTER
THE T800 TERMINATOR, *TERMINATOR 2*

IDENTIFYING POTENTIAL TROUBLE
EVIL! PURE AND SIMPLE, FROM THE 8TH DIMENSION!
BUCKAROO BANZAI, *THE ADVENTURES OF BUCKAROO BANZAI ACROSS THE 8TH DIMENSION*

FEELING SUPERIOR
EVEN AMONG MISFITS, YOU'RE MISFITS!
YUKON CORNELIUS, *RUDOLPH THE RED-NOSED REINDEER*

CHOOSING A FILM EXPERIENCE
COMING SOON:
DUDE, WHERE'S MY CAR II
THE SEARCH CONTINUES
BE AFRAID. BE VERY AFRAID.
VERONICA QUAIFE, *THE FLY* (1986 REMAKE)

ADVANCED TIPS

1) VOCALLY IMITATING THE SPEAKER OF THE ORIGINAL QUOTE IS THE SINCEREST FORM OF FANNERY!

2) TAKE THE SUBJECT NOUN IN A QUOTE AND REPLACE IT TO ADAPT TO YOUR NEEDS. FOR EXAMPLE: INSTEAD OF, "IN SPACE NO ONE CAN HEAR YOU SCREAM." (AD CAMPAIGN SLOGAN, ***ALIEN***), YOU COULD SAY, "IN ***NOISELAND ARCADE***, NO ONE CAN HEAR YOU SCREAM."

WORST TWO PAGE FILLER ***EVER***? I THINK ***NOT***!

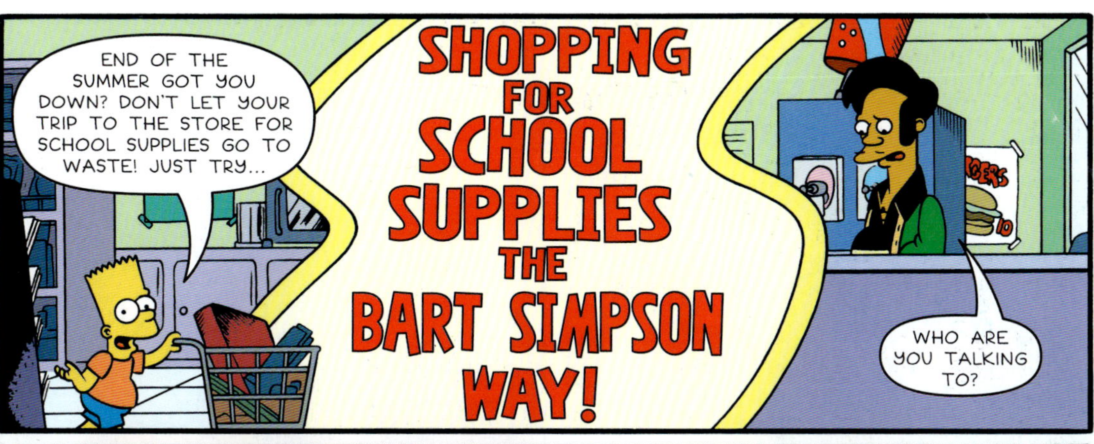

END OF THE SUMMER GOT YOU DOWN? DON'T LET YOUR TRIP TO THE STORE FOR SCHOOL SUPPLIES GO TO WASTE! JUST TRY...
SHOPPING FOR SCHOOL SUPPLIES THE BART SIMPSON WAY!
WHO ARE YOU TALKING TO?

A BIG BINDER MAKES YOU LOOK LIKE A DORK, RIGHT? ***WRONG!***

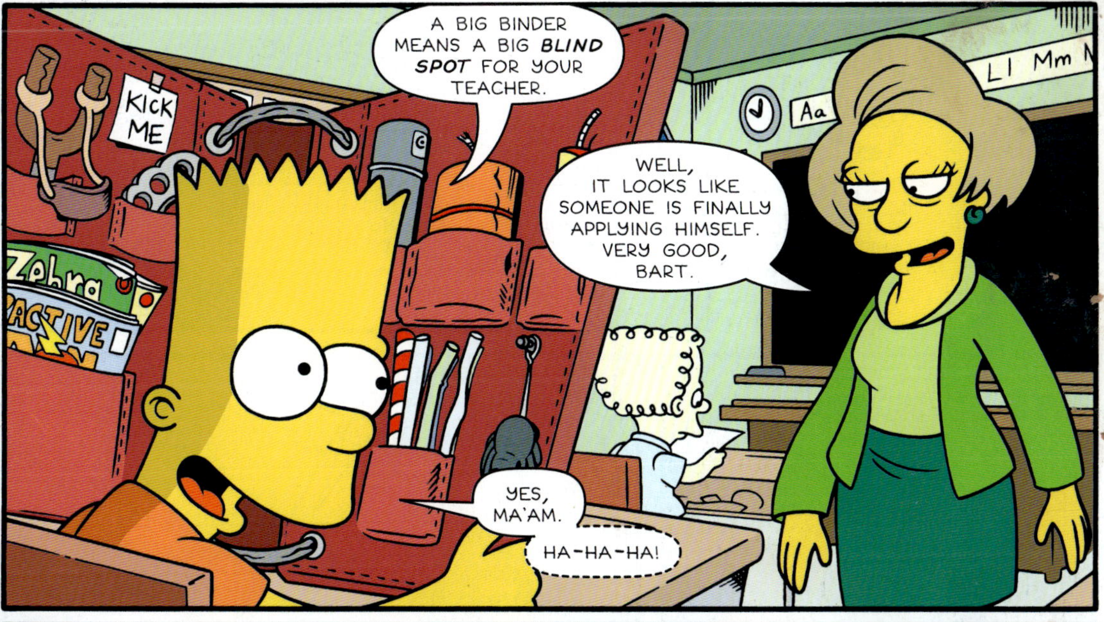

A BIG BINDER MEANS A BIG ***BLIND SPOT*** FOR YOUR TEACHER.
KICK ME
WELL, IT LOOKS LIKE SOMEONE IS FINALLY APPLYING HIMSELF. VERY GOOD, BART.
YES, MA'AM.
HA-HA-HA!

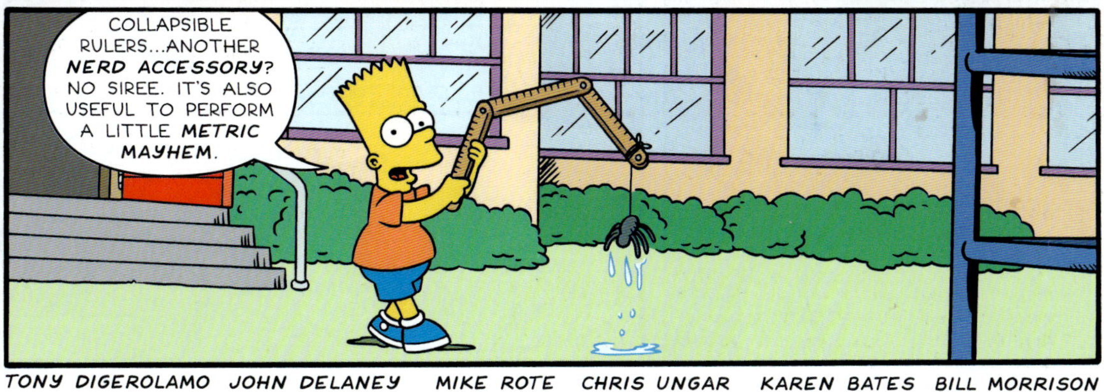

COLLAPSIBLE RULERS...ANOTHER ***NERD ACCESSORY?*** NO SIREE. IT'S ALSO USEFUL TO PERFORM A LITTLE ***METRIC MAYHEM***.

TONY DIGEROLAMO SCRIPT *JOHN DELANEY* PENCILS *MIKE ROTE* INKS *CHRIS UNGAR* COLORS *KAREN BATES* LETTERS *BILL MORRISON* EDITOR

BART, YOU'VE PULLED THIS PRANK A THOUSAND TIMES. DON'T YOU HAVE ANY **NEW** MATERIAL?
AS A MATTER OF FACT, I DO. BEFORE I PUT THE SPIDER ON THE STRING, I HAD IT IN MY **MOUTH**.

SPLAT!
EWWW!
AAAAH!

NEED SOMETHING TO DO DURING RECESS? JUST GLUE TWO PROTRACTORS TOGETHER AND YOU'VE GOT A **NERD-CHUCKER**. DWEEBS WON'T KNOW WHAT HIT 'EM.

OW! I THOUGHT **ANGLES** WERE MY FRIEND!
KA-CHUCK!

FINALLY, THE MOST BASIC SCHOOL SUPPLY HAS THE MOST EXCELLENT USE OF ALL! BY HOOKING ENOUGH PAPER CLIPS TOGETHER...

...YOU CAN MAKE AN **ESCAPE**!
SIMPSON?!
I GOTTA GO. JUST REMEMBER, WHEN BUYING SCHOOL SUPPLIES, **LEARNING** NEVER HAS TO INTERFERE WITH **FUN**!
THE END

TONY DIGEROLAMO SCRIPT · *JAMES LLOYD* PENCILS · *ANDREW PEPOY* INKS · *NATHAN HAMILL* COLORS · *KAREN BATES* LETTERS · *BILL MORRISON* EDITOR

OKAY, MAGS. READY FOR YOUR SURPRISE?
WALL E. WEASEL'S? OH, YEAH...THE OTHER PLACE WAS TOO EXPENSIVE. WELL, YOU WON'T KNOW THE DIFFERENCE, WILL YOU, YA LITTLE IDIOT?
WALL E. WEASEL'S
"WE CRAM FUN DOWN YOUR THROAT"
GOO-GA! AH, HA, HEE-HEE!

:SIGH: WELCOME TO WALL E. WEASEL'S, NO SHIRTS, NO SHOES, NO SUNDAES. PLEASE TAKE A SEAT IN WALLY'S PIZZALAND.
YEAH-YEAH, WE DON'T WANT NONE OF YER CRAPPY PIZZA. WE JUST CAME FOR THE INDOOR PLAY-GROUND.

SORRY, THE PLAYGROUND'S BEEN RESERVED BY ***THE DUCHESS OF DORINIA***.
OUT OF MY WAY!
OOF. I HAVE AN OWIE INSIDE ME.

LATER...
I'M SORRY, ANGEL. I JUST WANTED TO SURPRISE YOU TODAY. AW JEEZ, THIS IS JUST LIKE THE LAST TIME I TRIED TO SURPRISE YA...
ARE YOU CRAZY?! GET THAT BABY OUT OF HERE!
MY KID'S OLDER THAN THAT, AND I DON'T LET *HIM* PLAY!
INDOOR PAINT-BALL ARENA
DUDE, I DON'T SHOOT AT BABIES... ANYMORE.
FINE! WE'LL GO, YA BUNCH OF ELITIST SNOBS!

I FEEL LIKE SUCH A BABYSITTIN' FAILURE. I'M SORRY, MAGS.
SUCK! SUCK!

CLICK!
HEY, WHAT HAPPENED? DID I GO BLIND WITH GRIEF?

THE DUCHESS IS *GONE!*
I BREATHED MY BOOGERS.

CALM DOWN, LITTLE MINORS. MAGGIE AND MOE ARE ON THE CASE!
IN YOUR DREAMS!
YOU'RE NOT THE ONLY BARTENDER-TURNED-BABYSITTER THAT SOLVES MYSTERIES WITH A BABY!
HOLY GEEZ! IT'S TITANIA WITH THAT BABY GERALD KID!
AS SOON AS I STOP STARIN' AT YOUR BIG RACK THERE, WE'RE GONNA SOLVE THIS MYSTERY!
I HAVE ANOTHER OWIE.
THE DUCHESS'S TIARA! WE WIN! MYSTERY SOLVED!
WAIT A SECOND!
GERALD FOUND ANOTHER THING!
IN THE MYSTERY BIZ, THE TECHNICAL TERM IS "MYSTERY THING."
THAT'S A CLUE! EVEN I KNOW THAT!

THAT LOOKS LIKE FUR, BUT THE DUCHESS AIN'T COVERED WITH NO FUR! ONLY ONE GUY IN THIS PLACE GOT "MYSTERY THING" ALL OVER HIM...

...WALL E. WEASEL!
HUH?

ALL RIGHT, YA GIANT RODENT, WHERE'S DA DUCHESS?!
I DON'T KNOW WHAT YOU'RE TALKIN' ABOUT! I JUST GOT OFF MY BREAK!
HERE'S THE DUCHESS!

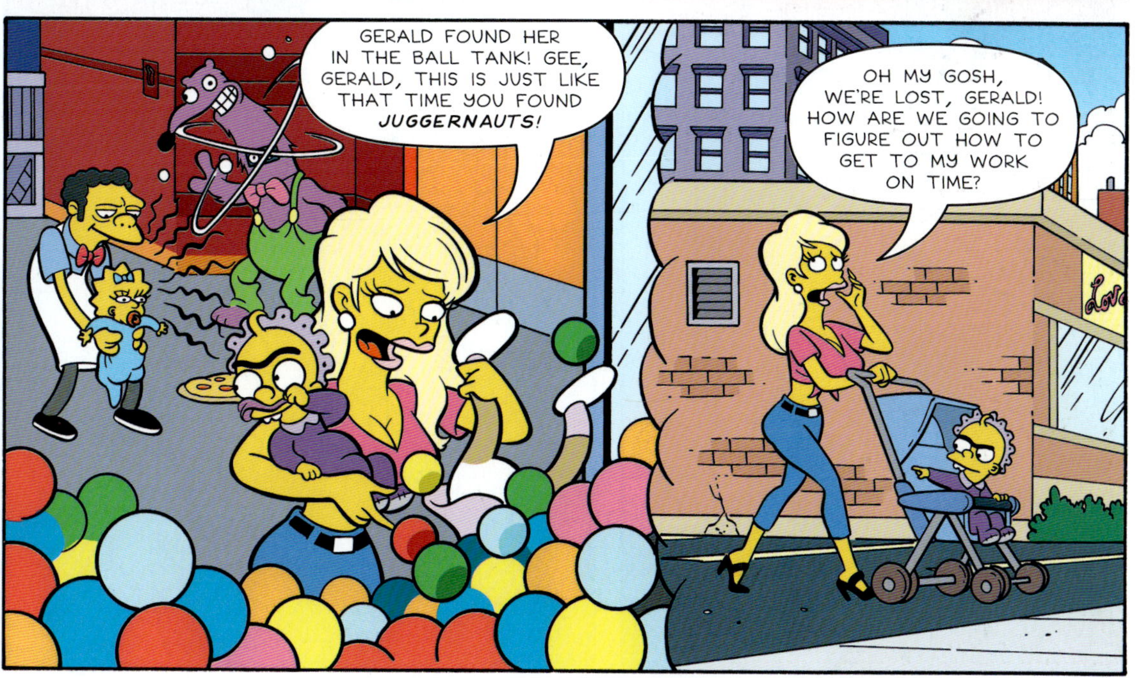
GERALD FOUND HER IN THE BALL TANK! GEE, GERALD, THIS IS JUST LIKE THAT TIME YOU FOUND JUGGERNAUTS!
OH MY GOSH, WE'RE LOST, GERALD! HOW ARE WE GOING TO FIGURE OUT HOW TO GET TO MY WORK ON TIME?

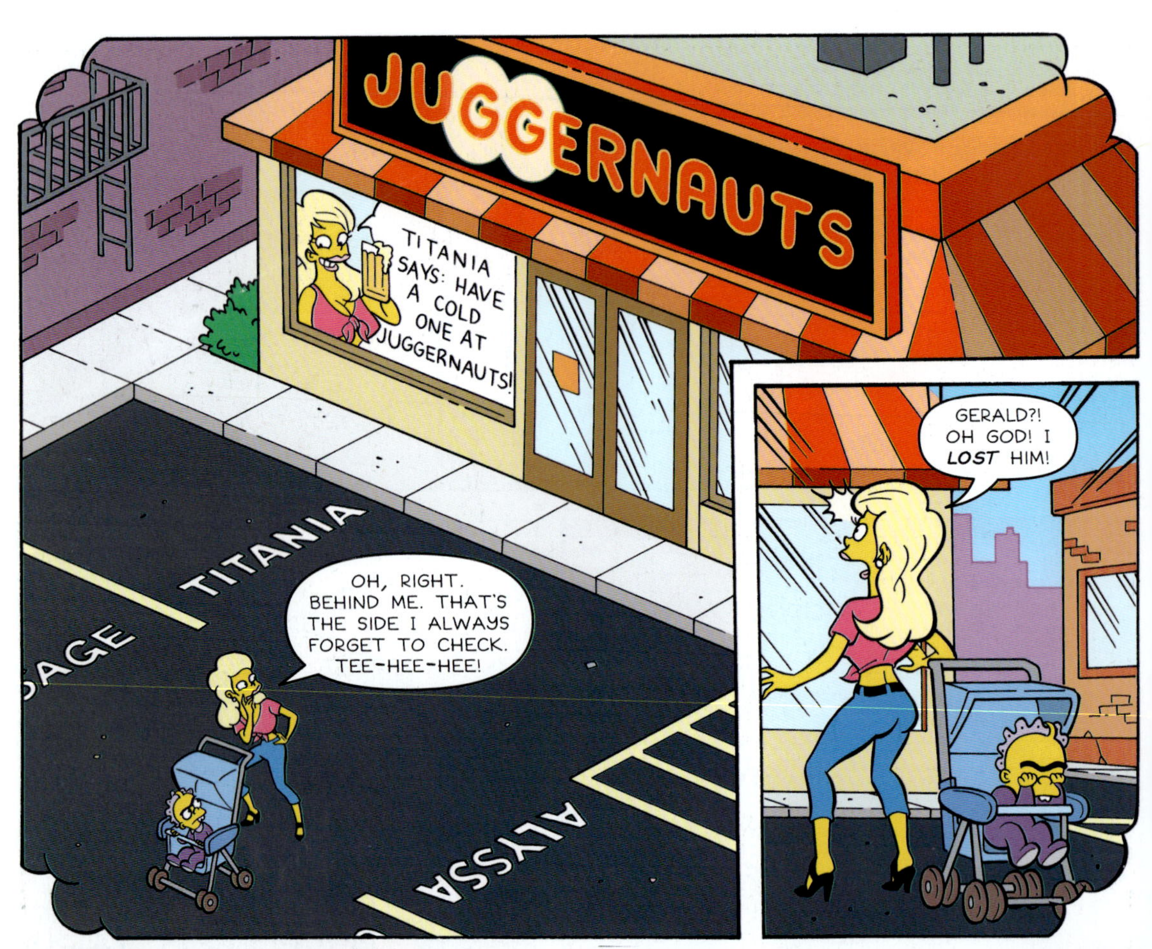
JUGGERNAUTS
TITANIA SAYS: HAVE A COLD ONE AT JUGGERNAUTS!
TITANIA
SAGE
ALYSSA
OH, RIGHT. BEHIND ME. THAT'S THE SIDE I ALWAYS FORGET TO CHECK. TEE-HEE-HEE!
GERALD?! OH GOD! I *LOST* HIM!

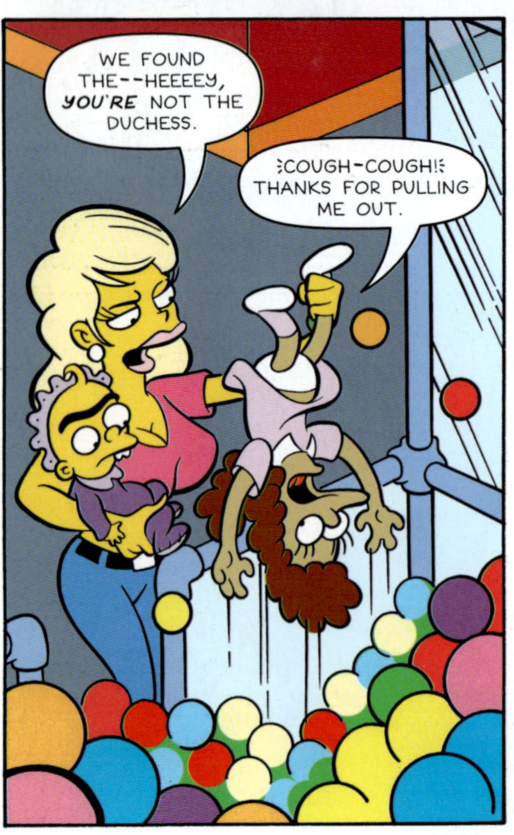
WE FOUND THE--HEEEEY, ***YOU'RE*** NOT THE DUCHESS.
COUGH-COUGH! THANKS FOR PULLING ME OUT.

GERALD! WHAT DO I DO? THIS IS HARDER THAN POURING A BEER.
WHOA!
?

A **SECOND** WALL E. WEASEL? A **CLONE!**

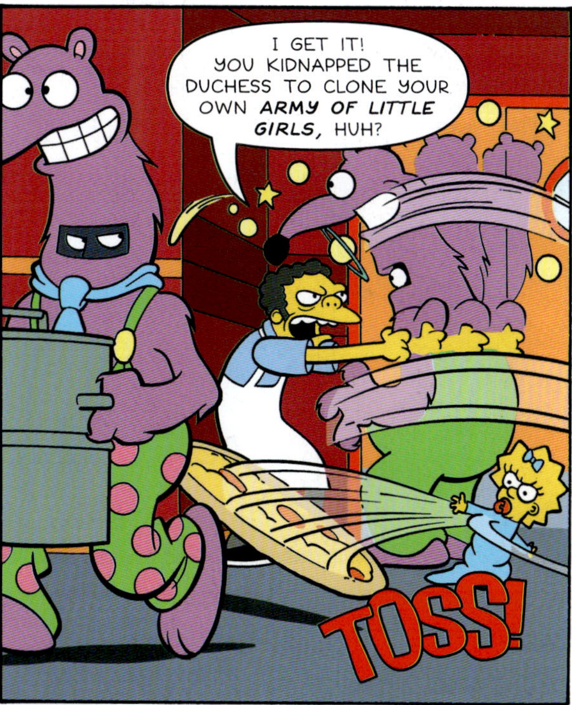
I GET IT! YOU KIDNAPPED THE DUCHESS TO CLONE YOUR OWN **ARMY OF LITTLE GIRLS**, HUH?
TOSS!

WHOA!
EEEK!
TRIP!

PACK RAT
HI! LINDSEY NAEGLE, CASTING DIRECTOR.
YOU KIDNAPPED ME!
I PREFER TO CALL IT "CHILD APPROPRIATION."

WHY YA APPROPRIATIN' THE DUCHESS THERE?
ARE YOU KIDDING? SHE'S *PURE EVIL!* AND THAT KIND OF "PARIS HILTON BAD-ITUDE" WILL SELL A LOT OF CHILDREN'S CLOTHES. DEMOGRAPHICS DON'T LIE.

LADY, I DON'T THINK YOU'LL BE SELLIN' NUTHIN'.
WHY DO YOU SAY THAT?

OH, RIGHT...THE KIDNAPPING.
THANKS TO MAGGIE AND MOE, THE ONLY THING YOU'LL BE KIDNAPPING IS JAIL!
UH...THAT DOESN'T MAKE ANY SENSE, CHIEF.

LATER...
I'M SORRY I RUINED TODAY, CUTIE. I WANTED TODAY TO BE LIKE A FANCY MIXED DRINK, BUT, INSTEAD, ALL I DID WAS SERVE YA ONE OF THOSE DOMESTIC BEERS I WATER DOWN FOR YER DAD.
"WE CRAM FU DOWN YOUR THROAT"
SUCK!
SUCK!

AW. NEXT TIME, WE'LL SOLVE A MYSTERY AT A RESTAURANT WITH BETTER FOOD. AT LEAST THERE WON'T BE NO TITANIA OR GERALD.

THAT'S IT! THAT'S IT! OH, YOU'RE SO BAD!
FWASH!

WORK IT, GERALD, WORK IT! MAKE ME LOVE YOU! NOW MAKE ME HATE YOU!
WOW, GERALD! I CAN'T BELIEVE YOU GOT THE JOB AS A CLOTHING MODEL!

PAF!
THE ONLY THING I CAN'T UNDERSTAND IS WHY YOU'RE NOT STILL IN JAIL.
I BROKE OUT! AND MY FORMER CELL-MATES ARE PERFECT FOR A NEW LINE OF COSMETICS FOR THE INCARCERATED! TALK ABOUT BAD-ITUDE!
THE END

PRESENTING EASTERN EUROPE'S FAVORITE CARTOON CAT AND MOUSE TEAM

WORKER AND PARASITE!

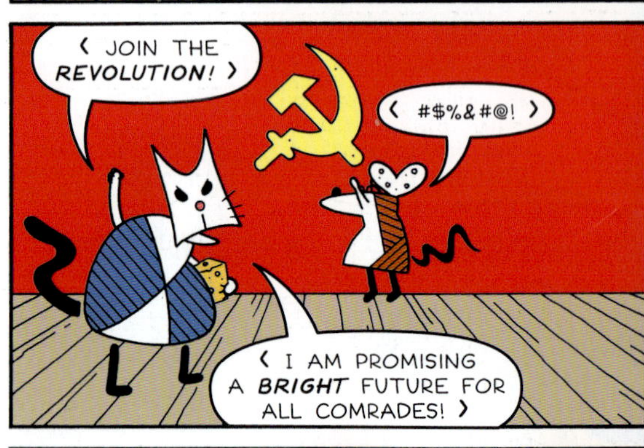

JESSE MCCANN SCRIPT | *MIKE ROTE* PENCILS & INKS | *NATHAN HAMILL* COLOR | *KAREN BATES* LETTERS | *BILL MORRISON* EDITOR

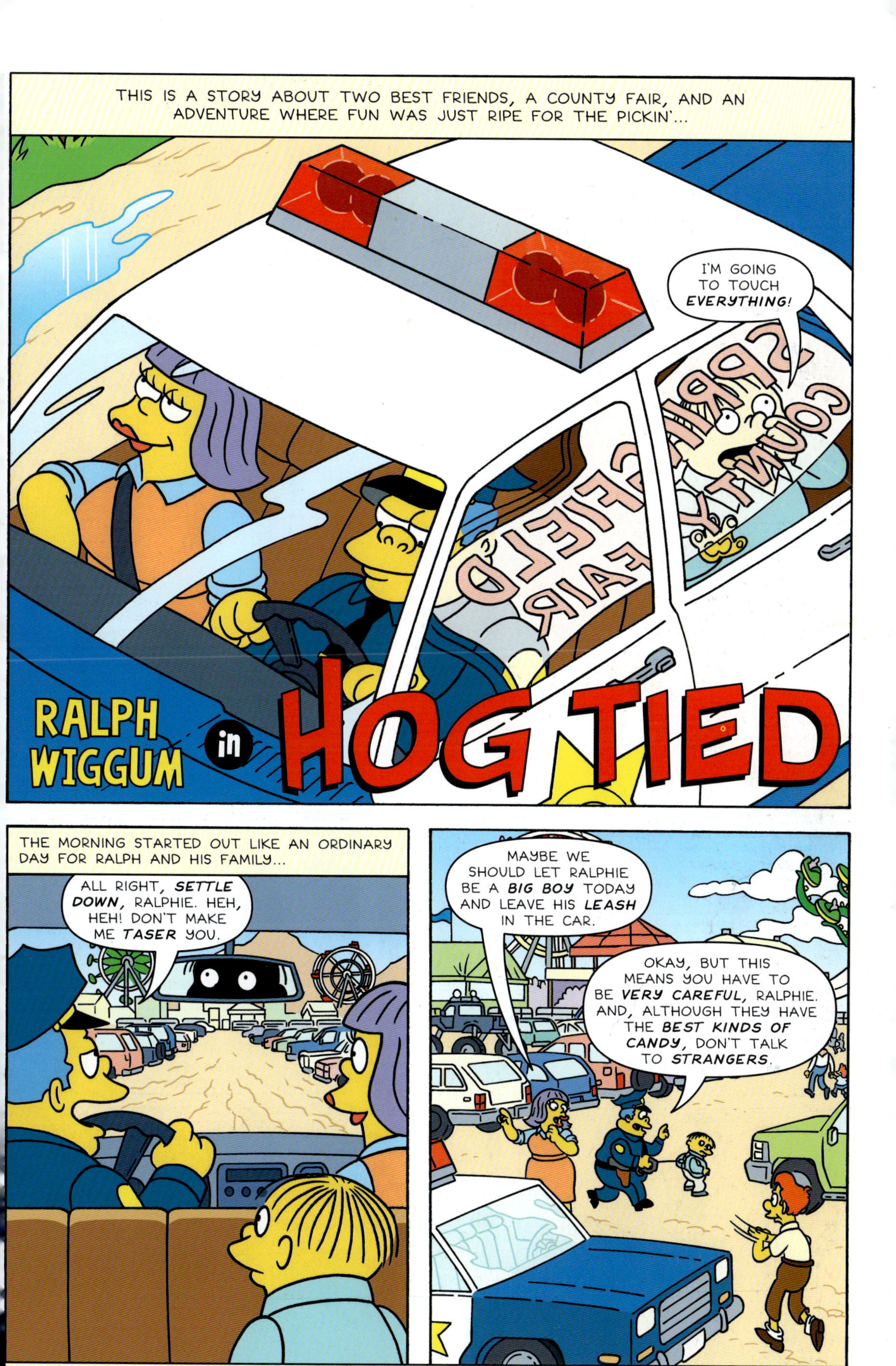

THIS IS A STORY ABOUT TWO BEST FRIENDS, A COUNTY FAIR, AND AN ADVENTURE WHERE FUN WAS JUST RIPE FOR THE PICKIN'...
I'M GOING TO TOUCH EVERYTHING!
SPRINGFIELD COUNTY FAIR
RALPH WIGGUM in HOG TIED
THE MORNING STARTED OUT LIKE AN ORDINARY DAY FOR RALPH AND HIS FAMILY...
ALL RIGHT, SETTLE DOWN, RALPHIE. HEH, HEH! DON'T MAKE ME TASER YOU.
MAYBE WE SHOULD LET RALPHIE BE A BIG BOY TODAY AND LEAVE HIS LEASH IN THE CAR.
OKAY, BUT THIS MEANS YOU HAVE TO BE VERY CAREFUL, RALPHIE. AND, ALTHOUGH THEY HAVE THE BEST KINDS OF CANDY, DON'T TALK TO STRANGERS.

AMANDA MCCANN SCRIPT · *JAMES LLOYD* PENCILS · *HOWARD SHUM* INKS · *ART VILLANUEVA* COLORS · *KAREN BATES* LETTERS · *BILL MORRISON* EDITOR

AS YOUR...ER, AH...MAYOR, I WOULD LIKE TO WELCOME THE PEOPLE OF...ER, AH...SPRINGFIELD TO THE COUNTY FAIR, AND REMIND YOU THAT THE PIE-EATING CONTEST IS AT FOUR O'CLOCK.
CRITTER'S FER YOR NOGGIN
AGNES' KRAFTS
DEEP-FRIED STUFF ON A STICK!
Android's Dungeon

HERE YOU GO, **RALPHIE**! HAVE FUN AND REMEMBER, A **STRANGER** IS A PERSON WHO DOESN'T KNOW YOUR NAME.
LET'S GO, HONEY. I HAVE GOT TO GET ME ONE OF THOSE ***DEEP-FRIED PIES ON A STICK!***

HI! YOU'RE ***OLDER*** BOYS.

YOINK! WE'LL BE ***TAKING*** THIS. THANKS, DWEEB!

NOW I CAN GET THAT ***MACE*** I WANTED.
AWESOME!
SCORE!
THOSE BOYS ARE LIKE WHEN ***CHURCH*** COMES TO THE DOOR.

RALPH WASN'T GOING TO LET A FEW BULLIES RUIN HIS GOOD TIME...
OOOH!
LOOK AT ME, LISA! I'M DAVY CROCKETT!
I THINK WEARING POOR DEAD ANIMALS ON YOUR HEAD IS DISGUSTING!
WAIT A MINUTE, BART! I DON'T THINK IT'S DEAD!
GRRRR!
AAAAH!

MY HAT BLOWS BUBBLES!
SHUDDER!
DERN CRITTER! I DONE ALREADY KILT YOU ONCE WITH MAH GAS BUGGY!

YEP, NOT EVEN A RABID CRITTER COULD SPOIL RALPH'S DAY...
HELLO, MR. PIXIE! WAIT FOR ME!

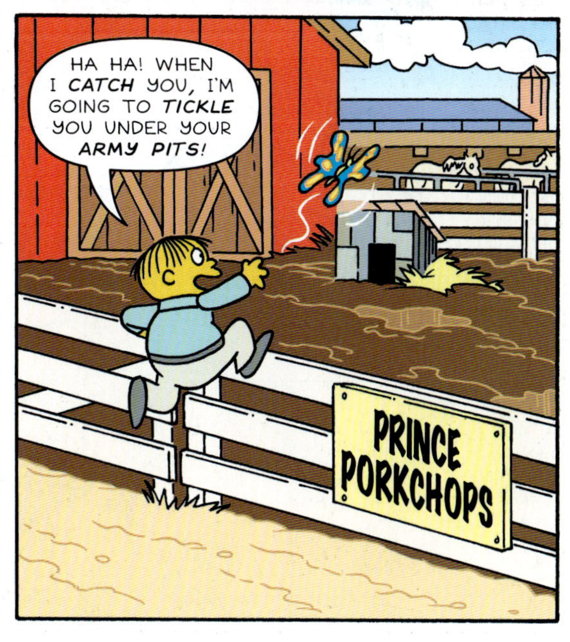
HA HA! WHEN I CATCH YOU, I'M GOING TO TICKLE YOU UNDER YOUR ARMY PITS!
PRINCE PORKCHOPS

HEE HEE! MY FINGERS ARE GOING TO GET YOU!
CLICK-CLACK!

SPLORT!

I'M GOING TO MAKE A BROWN ANGEL!

OH, H-HI. YOU'RE PRINCE PORKCHOPS! I SEED IT ON THE GATE.
YOU'RE NOT A STRANGER, 'CAUSE I KNOW YOUR NAME.
SNORT!

POUNCE
SNIFF!
SNIFF!
STOP! THE WIND FROM YOUR BOOGIE HOLES IS TICKLING ME!
SNIFF!
SNORT!

♪ I'M FOLLOWING ♪ THE LEADER...THE LEADER...THE ♪ LEADER! ♪

SO, RALPH AND THE PRINCE WERE LIKE TWO VERY MUDDY PEAS IN A POD...
GORGING...
IT'S LIKE EASTER AT GRANDMA'S!

FROLICKING...
IT'S SNOWING TICKLE STICKS!

DISCOVERING...
THAT IS SOME PIG

YOU'RE FREE MR. PIXIE! FLY BACK TO FERNGULLY!

AND, OF COURSE, RELAXING...
WE'RE GOING TO BE BEST FRIENDS FOREVER, PRINCE PORKCHOPS, AND I AM GOING TO MAKE YOU A BRACELET THAT SAYS SO!

AS THE...ER, AH...WINNER OF THE PIE-EATING CONTEST, I AWARD YOU WITH THE...ER, AH...DELICIOUS PRINCE PORKCHOPS.
YIPPEE! THIS HERE IS THE SECOND BEST DAY OF MAH LIFE!*
DADDY, I'M PLAYING IN THE WET SANDBOX!
RALPHIE!
*THE BEST DAY OF CLETUS' LIFE WAS WHEN HE FOUND OUT HIS LEG WASN'T GANGRENOUS, IT HAD JUST FALLEN ASLEEP IN A PLATE OF LIME JELL-O.

YOU HAVE A DATE WITH MAH SUPPER TABLE!
SNORT!

THERE YOU ARE, RALPHIE! WHOO-WEE! LET'S GET YOU HOME FOR A BATH.
SNORT!

BACK AT HOME...
C'MON, RALPHIE! THIS IS YOUR FAVORITE PART OF THE DAY!
GRUNT!
SNORT!
REMEMBER? YOU'RE A MERBOY, AND I'M THE CAPTAIN OF A JAMAICAN CRUISE SHIP, TRYING TO HARPOON YOU!

OH, MY EYES! I-I'M TEMPORARILY BLINDED!
REEE!
SPLOOSH!

WHAT HAS GOTTEN INTO YOU, SON?
LET'S JUST GET YOU IN YOUR JAMMIES, AND I'LL TELL YOU A BEDTIME STORY.

SO, THE WOLF GOES TO THE **SECOND PIG'S HOUSE,** WHICH IS MADE OF **POPSICLE STICKS**...

AND THE WOLF **HUFFED** AND **PUFFED** AND **BLEW** THE PIG'S HOUSE DOWN! **WHOOSH!**
THE LITTLE PIGGY **SQUEALED**...
SQUEAL!

SAY, THAT'S A **PRETTY GOOD** PIG NOISE, RALPHIE... ALMOST TOO GOOD.
WAIT A SECOND!

YOU'RE **NOT** MY **RALPHIE!**
OINK!

IF I TOOK **YOU** HOME **INSTEAD** OF RALPHIE, THEN HE'S...**OH NO,** I'VE MADE A **TERRIBLE** MISTAKE!
THAT YOKEL IS GOING TO **EAT MY SON!**

THREE **MINOR COLLISIONS** LATER, THE CHIEF ARRIVED AT **CLETUS' SHACK**...
I HOPE I'M NOT **TOO LATE,** OR SARAH IS GOING TO BE **SO** MAD AT ME!

FREEZE, HILLBILLY! THAT PORKER IS NO PIG!
FIRST BRANDINE TOOK MY CHILLIN' AWAY IN THE NIGHT, AND NOW THIS!
BASH!
HI, DADDY! I'M A TABLE LEG!

OH, GREAT LEAPIN' CANNIBALS...HEH, HEH... YOU'RE NOT BEING EATEN!
YOU REALLY GAVE ME A SCARE RALPHIE!

AW, DANG.
CAN THE PRINCE BE MY NEW BROTHER AND SLEEP IN MY CLOSET?
GEE, I DON'T KNOW, RALPHIE... HEH, HEH! UH, HE SURE IS A CUTE LITTLE FELLA.
CRASH!

WELL, IT LOOKS LIKE EVERYBODY WINS.
YEP, EVERYONE IS HAPPY.
ALL OF US.
OOOH. I DONE ATE ALL THEM PIES IN VAIN.

BACK AT THE WIGGUM HOME, EVERYTHING WAS AS IT SHOULD BE...
AWW, LOOK AT THOSE TWO, HAVING THE TIME OF THEIR LIVES. THE BEST THINGS IN LIFE REALLY ARE FREE.
OOH, I THINK MY SUPPER WANTS TO BE ON THE OUTSIDE AGAIN.
THE END

BART SIMPSON in CLONE ALONE
MARY TRAINOR SCRIPT
MIKE DECARLO PENCILS
PHYLLIS NOVIN INKS
NATHAN HAMILL COLORS
KAREN BATES LETTERS
BILL MORRISON EDITOR

LIKEWISE.
DITTO.

MAN, I SURE WISH THERE WERE TWO OF ME!

HEY! WHAT'S THIS?
HEY, KIDS! I DOUBLE DARE YOU TO BUY MY
FANTASTIC CLONE AT HOME KIT!
RADIOACTIVE MAN

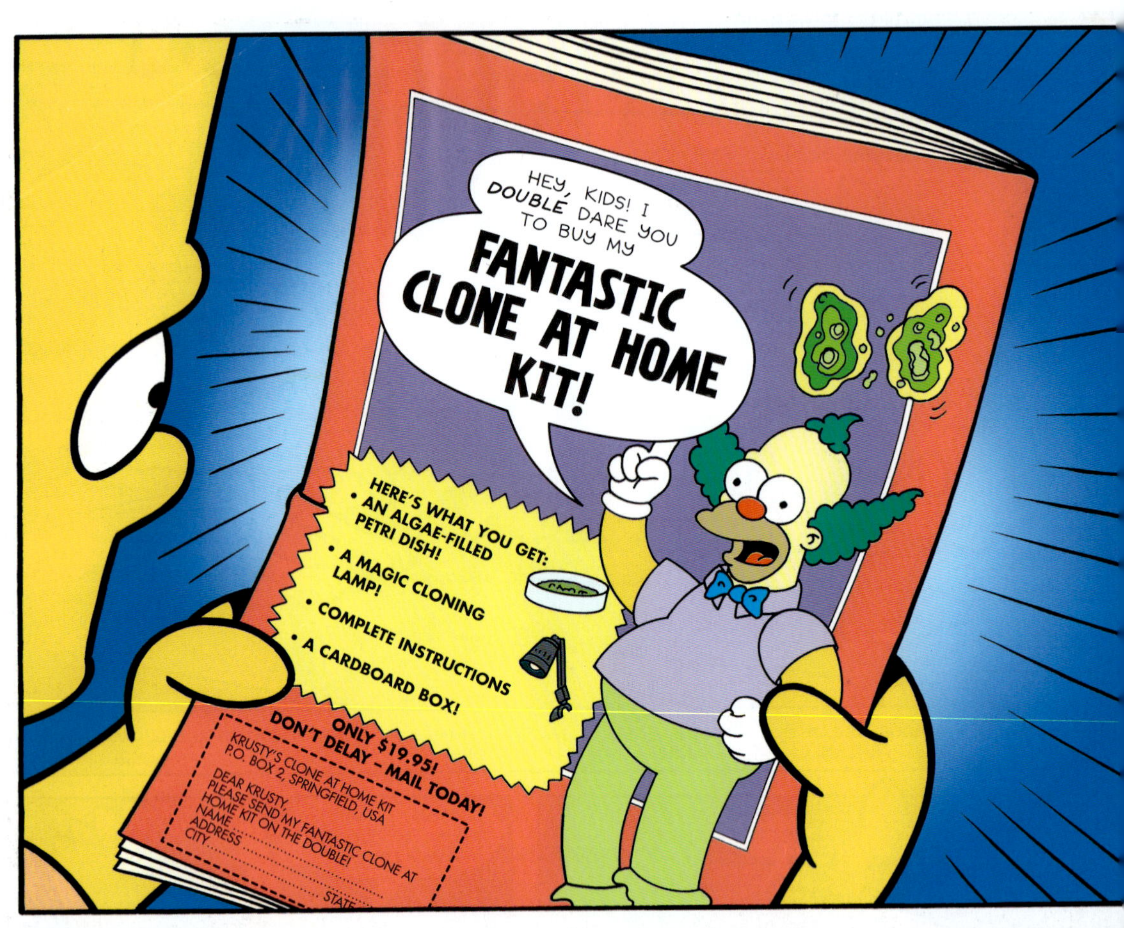
HEY, KIDS! I DOUBLE DARE YOU TO BUY MY
FANTASTIC CLONE AT HOME KIT!
HERE'S WHAT YOU GET:
• AN ALGAE-FILLED PETRI DISH!
• A MAGIC CLONING LAMP!
• COMPLETE INSTRUCTIONS
• A CARDBOARD BOX!
ONLY $19.95!
DON'T DELAY – MAIL TODAY!
KRUSTY'S CLONE AT HOME KIT
P.O. BOX 2, SPRINGFIELD, USA
DEAR KRUSTY,
PLEASE SEND MY FANTASTIC CLONE AT HOME KIT ON THE DOUBLE!
NAME
ADDRESS
CITY
STATE

WHOA! I'M SENDING AWAY FOR KRUSTY'S FANTASTIC CLONE AT HOME KIT RIGHT NOW!
RADIOACTIVE MAN

SIX TO EIGHT WEEKS LATER...
OH, BABY! THIS IS *IT*!
CLONE AT HOME KIT

LET'S SEE...
"SCRAPE SOME CELLS FROM INSIDE YOUR CHEEK..."

"...AND PUT THOSE CELLS IN THE ENCLOSED PETRI DISH. LEAVE OVERNIGHT UNDER THE MAGIC CLONING LAMP."

THAT NIGHT...
ZZZZZZZ
MAGIC CLONING LAMP

THE NEXT MORNING...
YAWN

HEY, MAN, NICE ROOM!
COOL!

SO, WHAT DO YOU WANT TO DO?

I DUNNO. WHAT DO **YOU** WANT TO DO?

HEY, I KNOW! LET'S FOOL LISA. I'LL GO DOWNSTAIRS, AND YOU WAIT HERE.
NO. **I'LL** GO DOWNSTAIRS. **YOU** WAIT HERE.

NO, **YOU** WAIT HERE.
NO, **YOU** WAIT HERE.

HEY, LISTEN, MARY-KATE. **I'M** BART. **YOU'RE** THE CLONE.
NO, **YOU'RE** THE CLONE.

AM NOT.
ARE, TOO.

SHUT UP.
NO, **YOU** SHUT UP.

MAN, THIS CLONE IS A REAL PAIN IN THE BUTT.
NO, *YOU'RE* THE PAIN IN THE BUTT.

I THINK THIS IS WHAT THEY CALL *BUYER'S REMORSE*.

HEY! WHAT'S *THIS*?

WOO-HOO!
HEY, KIDS! IS YOUR CLONE A TOTAL PAIN IN YOUR BUTT? DO YOU LONG TO SAY GOOD-BYE FOREVER? DON'T SAY IT- *SPRAY IT*...WITH
CLONE B-GONE!
ONLY $19.95! DON'T WAIT! ACT NOW!
KRUSTY'S CLONE B-GONE
P.O. BOX 3, SPRINGFIELD, USA
DEAR KRUSTY,
PLEASE RUSH MY CLONE B-GONE PRONTO!
NAME
ADDRESS
CITY
STATE

SOMETIME LATER...
HEH, HEH!
CLONE B-GONE

MEANWHILE...
HEH, HEH!
BART B-GONE

♪ OH, ♪
♪ CLONE-EEE... ♪

BAM!

EEEEEYAAAAAH!!!

YIIIIII!!!

YIIIIIIII...

HEY! WAKE UP, BART! I'M HEADING OVER TO THE KWIK-E-MART FOR THE ***TWO-FOR-ONE*** AFTER SCHOOL SPECIAL.

COOL! ME, TWO. I MEAN, ME...TOO. I MEAN, ME ONE!

ME. THE ONE AND ONLY ME.
JUST ME.
MYSELF.
I ALONE.
SOLO MIO.

AH, WHAT FOOLS THESE MORTALS BE.
DITTO.
THE END

TO THE FINDER OF THIS FISH OF GOLD, GOOD LUCK TIMES THREE! BUT TO ANY WHO STEAL IT,
DOOM ON THEE...
DOOM ON THEE...
DOOM ON THEE!
MAGGIE SIMPSON in
BABY GOT BACK (AT BURNS)

CUT IT OUT, DAD! YOU'RE SCARING US!
GEEZ, I'M JUST SHOWING YOU THE MAGICAL GOLDEN FISH I FOUND.
SEE? IT SAYS RIGHT ON THE FISH, "DOOM ON THEE" THREE TIMES!

HOMER, I DOUBT THAT OLD FISH IS GOLD OR MAGIC.
PERHAPS ITS POWER WILL COME FROM THE GLOW OF A FULL MOON!
HRRRM...BART, DO YOU HAVE TO DO THAT EVERY TIME WE COME TO THE BEACH?
WHY RUIN A PERFECT RECORD?

JESSE MCCANN SCRIPT | JOHN COSTANZA PENCILS | HOWARD SHUM INKS | ART VILLANUEVA COLORS | KAREN BATES LETTERS | BILL MORRISON EDITOR

SOON...
WASN'T THAT A YUMMY LUNCH?
I DUNNO, MOM ⁝HUCK!⁝ I THINK I MAY HAVE SWALLOWED A BONE!
BART! YOU'LL GET KID SMELL ON IT!

LATER...
⁝YAWN!⁝ I'M GOING TO TAKE A NAP. PROTECT THE GOLDEN FISH, MARGE.
OOOOH! IT'S PRETTY HEAVY! MAYBE IT IS REAL GOLD.
LISA, KEEP AN EYE ON IT, WHILE I REST WITH YOUR FATHER.

LISTEN, BART, I CAME HERE TO PRACTICE FOR THE SAND SCULPTURE CHAMPIONSHIP, AND YOU OWE ME FOR GIVING YOU ALL MY DESSERTS LAST WEEK!
JUST STAY HERE AND WATCH THE FISH!
OH, MAN! CURSE MY RAGING SWEET TOOTH!

HEY, MAGGIE, OLD PAL, OLD CHUM! YOU'LL GUARD THIS, SO I CAN GO WATCH THE TEENAGERS SMOKE BEHIND THE SNACK BAR, RIGHT?
SUCK! SUCK!
I KNEW YOU WOULD!

MOMENTS LATER...
ZZZZZ!

LOOK, SMITHERS, IT'S THAT CHILD WHO SHOT ME.
AND WHAT'S THIS? SOMEONE HAS ENTRUSTED HER WITH A PRICE-LESS GOLDEN ARTIFACT!

BEST TAKE IT...OOF... FOR SAFE-KEEPING... UNH...UNHAND IT, YOU RAGAMUFFIN...OOF! SHE HAS THE WRESTLER'S GRIP OF ED "STRANGLER" LEWIS HIMSELF!
PANT! YOU FETCH IT, SMITHERS!
TAKE SOMETHING FROM A SLEEPING CHILD, SIR?

IF YOU DO, WAYLON, YOU'LL COME TO REGRET IT!
OHHH!
COME ON...LIVE A LITTLE! BREAK OUT OF YOUR SHELL!
POOF!
POOF!

JUST DO IT, YOU IDIOT!
GASP!
POOF!

SORRY, MAGGIE. I'LL MAKE IT UP TO YOU... SOMEHOW.

A SHORT WHILE LATER...
THAT GOLDEN FISH WAS GONNA BRING US GOOD LUCK! THANKS A LOT, MAGGIE! NOW, WHO KNOWS WHERE IT WENT?!
I CAN'T BELIEVE POOPY-PANTS TOOK HER EYES OFF THE PRIZE!
BABIES ARE SO UNRELIABLE!
UHN-UHN!

THAT EVENING...
SIGH!

GREAT! NOW I HAVE TO GET GOLD POLISH FOR THE STOLEN FISH!
ANH?

FIP!

FWISH!
PERHAPS A LITTLE MUSIC WILL SOOTHE MY STRESSED NERVES.

KLUMP!
♪ KNOCK ♪ THREE TIMES... ON THE CEILING IF YOU WAAAAANT ♪ ME! ♫

♫ TWICE ON ♪ THE PIPES...IF THE ANSWER IS ♪ NOOOOOO! ♪

HERE'S YOUR BOTTLE OF GOLD POLISH, MR. BURNS!
TONIGHT I HAVE A MEETING OF THE CRIMEAN WAR VETS, SMITHERS! I CAN'T WAIT AROUND FOR YOU!
A TOOTHBRUSH, A LITTLE BAKING SODA, AND GOOD OLD FASHIONED ELBOW GREASE DID THE TRICK!
BY THE WAY, YOU NEED A NEW TOOTH-BRUSH.

NOW, LET'S SEE WHAT OUR NEWFOUND FRIEND HERE SAYS. "TO THE FINDER OF THIS FISH..." YES..."GOOD LUCK..." YES, YES...

"BUT TO ANY WHO STEAL IT..." OH, DEAR...
"DOOM..." OH, DEAR! "DOOM...DOOM!"
BY THE LOCK ON PANDORA'S BOX, SMITHERS! THIS IS A CURSED FISH!

"OOOO! THERE'S AN ILL WIND COMING OUR WAY BECAUSE OF THIS FISH, SMITHERS! AN ILL WIND INDEED!"
SUCK!
SUCK!
SUCK!

SUCK!
SUCK!
SUCK?

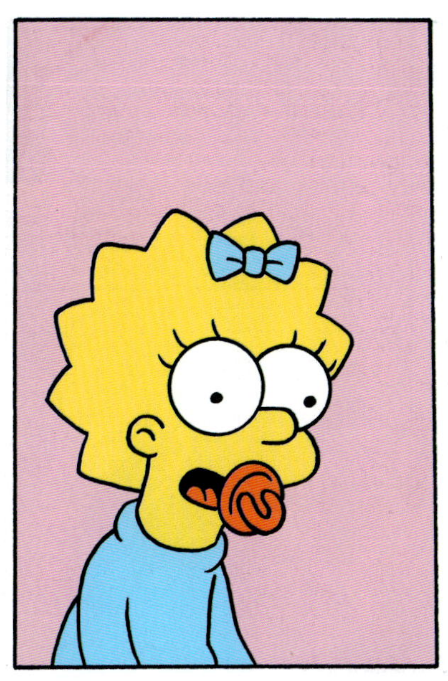

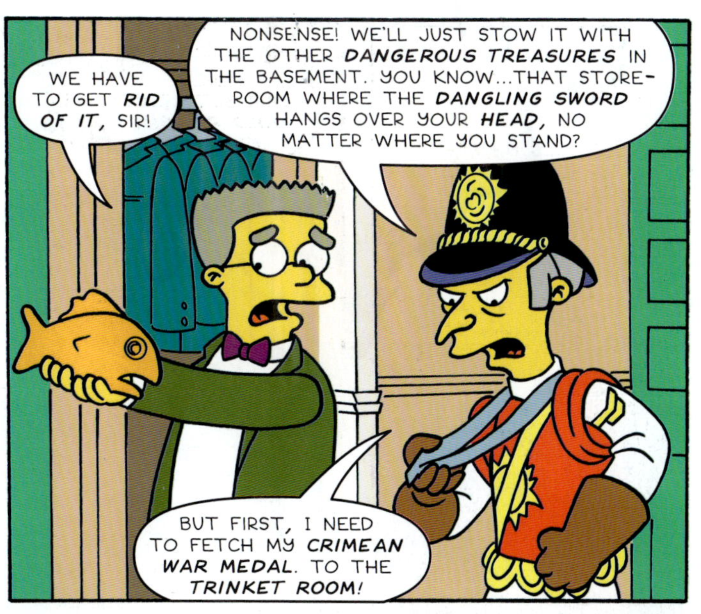
WE HAVE TO GET RID OF IT, SIR!
NONSENSE! WE'LL JUST STOW IT WITH THE OTHER DANGEROUS TREASURES IN THE BASEMENT. YOU KNOW...THAT STORE-ROOM WHERE THE DANGLING SWORD HANGS OVER YOUR HEAD, NO MATTER WHERE YOU STAND?
BUT FIRST, I NEED TO FETCH MY CRIMEAN WAR MEDAL. TO THE TRINKET ROOM!

WHAT, IN THE NAME OF DRUNKEN GARBO, WAS THAT NOISE?!
CRASH!
WHAT IF IT'S THE ANGRY CURSE, COME LOOKING FOR THE STOLEN FISH AND THE THIEVES THAT TOOK IT?

SUCK!
SUCK!
SUCK!
HMPH!

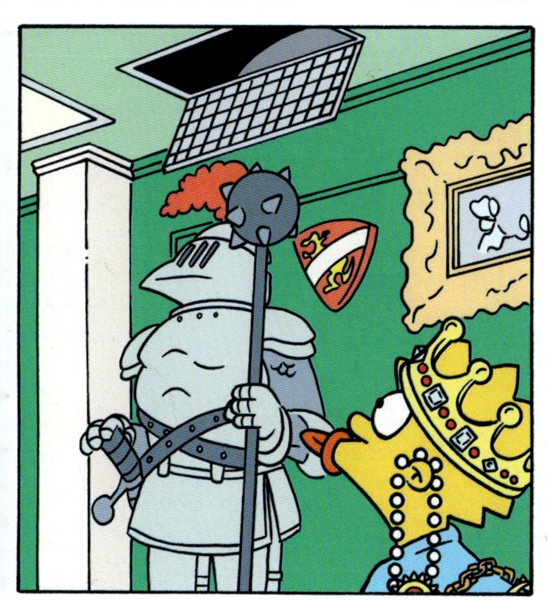

REALLY SMITHERS, YOU HAVE THE MOST VIVID IMAGINATION! THAT'S NOT HOW CURSES WORK.
I SHOULD KNOW. I'VE CAST QUITE A FEW ON BUSINESS PARTNERS IN MY TIME!
KREEEAK!

AAAAH! IT'S THE CURSE. IT'S BEGUN! LET ME TAKE IT BACK, MR. BURNS!
A BURNS NEVER GIVES BACK GOLD! NOW, LET'S GET MY CRIMEAN CROSS AND GET TO THE PARTY!
CLONG!

MINUTES PASS...
WHERE IS IT?! SMITHERS, YOU DIDN'T WEAR IT TO ONE OF YOUR SUNDAY AFTERNOON SPA PARTIES, DID YOU?
MR. BURNS, I WOULD NEVER TAKE SOMETHING OF YOURS.
WELL, IT DIDN'T JUST CRAWL OUT OF HERE!

THIS IS TERRIBLE, SMITHERS, TERRIBLE...THE WORST THING POSSIBLE!

DO YOU KNOW WHAT WILL HAPPEN IF I SHOW UP WITHOUT MY MEDAL? THE OTHERS WILL POOH-POOH ME, IN THE MOST UNFORGIVING OF WAYS!
I SAY, "POOH-POOH!"
INDEED. "POOH-POOH!"
"POOH... A-POOH!"

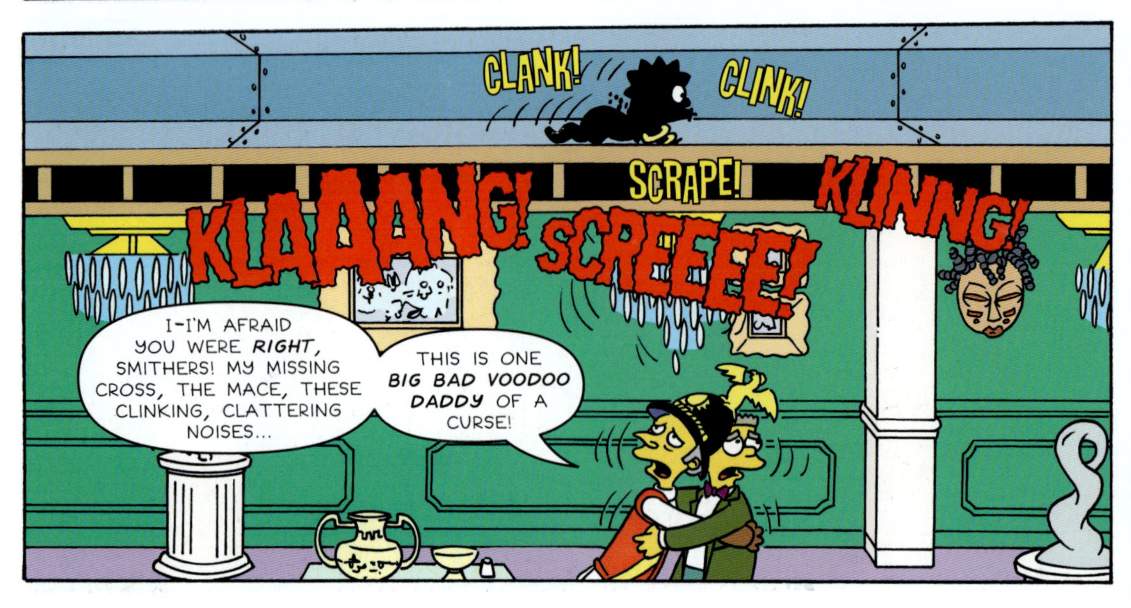
CLANK!
CLINK!
SCRAPE!
KLAAANG!
SCREEEE!
KLINNG!
I-I'M AFRAID YOU WERE RIGHT, SMITHERS! MY MISSING CROSS, THE MACE, THESE CLINKING, CLATTERING NOISES...
THIS IS ONE BIG BAD VOODOO DADDY OF A CURSE!

?

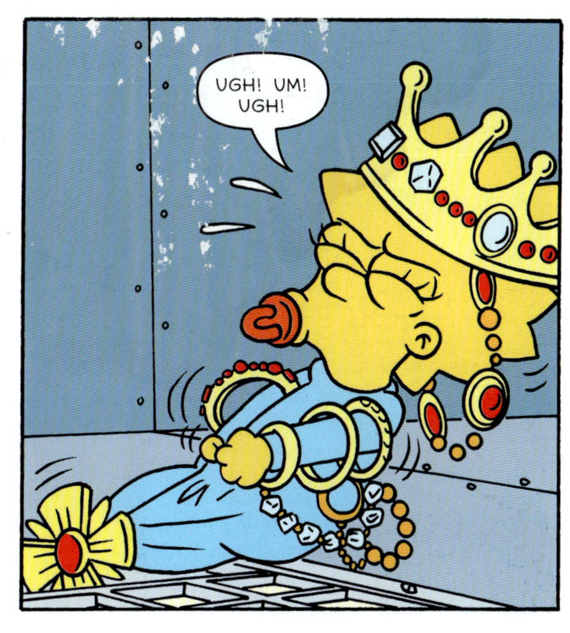
UGH! UM! UGH!

UUUUUGH! UUUUM!
IT'S GETTING ANGRIER!
MR. BURNS, AGREE TO GIVE BACK THE GOLD FISH! IT'S OUR ONLY HOPE!
OKAY, OKAY! I'LL...GIVE...IT... BACK...!
OOO! I HOPE YOU'RE HAPPY, SMITHERS! I ALMOST CHOKED ON MY OWN BILE SAYING THAT!

NOW THEN, MR. CURSE, WHAT ARE YOU GOING TO DO FOR ME IN RETURN?
MR. BURNS! IS IT WISE TO TEMPT FATE?!
A BURNS NEVER GIVES AWAY SOMETHING FOR FREE!

SUCK!
ZING!
TEAR!
CLANK!

PLINK!
FSSSSSSH!

TANG!
MING!
JIN!

THERE, YOU SEE, SMITHERS? QUID PRO QUO. I GIVE SOMETHING TO THE CURSE, IT GIVES ME SOMETHING BACK.
AU!
THUNK!

YAAAAA...I'LLBERIGHTBACK MR.BURNS,I'MJUSTGOINGTO RETURNTHEGOLDENFISHTO THESIMPSONS...AAAAAAH!
YES...FINE...MY! WHO'S THIS STRAPPING YOUNG INFANTRYMAN?
COLONEL MONTY BURNS, LADIES, AT YOUR SERVICE!

CRACK!
OH, GREAT.

...LO, THOUGH I WALK THROUGH THE VALLEY OF THE SHADOW OF DEATH...
CLUMP!

THERE, MAGGIE. I TOLD YOU I'D MAKE IT UP TO YOU.

SUCK! SUCK! SUCK!
I JUST HOPE IT'S ENOUGH!

THE NEXT MORNING...
I FEEL SO BAD ABOUT THE WAY I TREATED THE BABY YESTERDAY!
ME, TOO!
I DIDN'T TREAT HER BADLY, BUT I FEEL BADLY FOR HER.
AND I WAS HOPING TO GET IN A LITTLE MORE RIDICULE BEFORE PANCAKES!

YOWZA!
MARGE, DID I MENTION THAT MAGGIE IS MY FAVORITE CHILD?
HEY, WE'RE STANDING RIGHT HERE!
NO, HE'S RIGHT, LIS. MAGGIE'S THE BEST!
THE END

MATT G[illegible]NING presents

BART SIMPSON in FORT KNOCKS

CHECK THIS OUT, MILHOUSE.

MARY TRAINOR	CARLOS VALENTI	PHYLLIS NOVIN	NATHAN HAMILL	KAREN BATES	BILL MORRISON
SCRIPT	PENCILS	INKS	COLORS	LETTERS	EDITOR

TA-DA! A COOL FORT.

IT'S LIKE WE'RE INSIDE A REINFORCED BUNKER!

VROOOM! VROOOM!
WHAT'S THAT SOUND?

HUNKER DOWN, MEN! ENEMY AIRCRAFT APPROACHING!

VAROOOM!

FAH-LOOOMPH

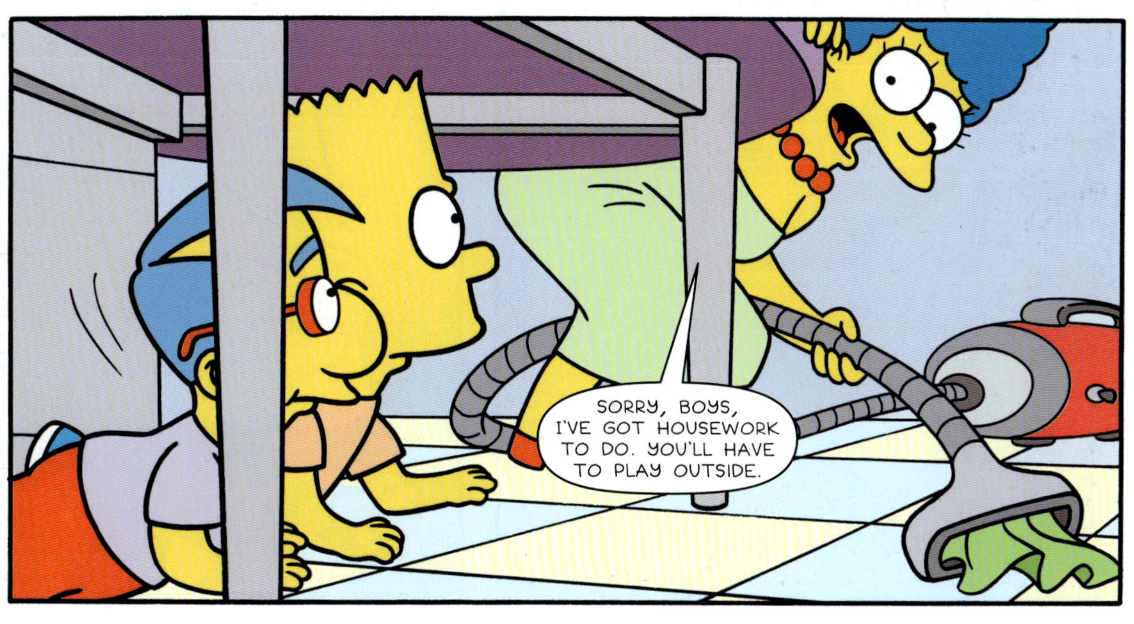
SORRY, BOYS, I'VE GOT HOUSEWORK TO DO. YOU'LL HAVE TO PLAY OUTSIDE.

MAN, THAT WAS SUCH A COOL FORT.

HEY, **LOOK!**

WOW! SOME LUCKY HOUSEWIFE JUST GOT A NEW 48" STAINLESS STEEL, SUB ZERO, SIDE-BY-SIDE REFRIGERATOR WITH 28 CUBIC FEET OF STORAGE!

HEY, YOU KNOW WHAT? THIS'LL MAKES **A COOL FORT!**

IT'S LIKE WE'RE DEEP INSIDE A MILITARY FORTRESS!

THUMP!
MORTAR FIRE! TAKE COVER!

THUMP! THUMP!

GET LOST, LITTLE GEEKS. WE'RE MAKING THIS OUR NEW **CLUB-HOUSE**.

HEY! WE WERE THE FIRST ONES HERE.
YEAH? AND NOW YOU'RE THE FIRST ONES TO LEAVE.

WHO CARES? THE TREEHOUSE IS A WAY BETTER FORT ANYHOW.
THAT'S NOT THE POINT. THIS IS ABOUT TURF.

WELL, THERE'S NOTHING WE CAN DO ABOUT IT NOW.
OH, YEAH?

DUDES! THAT WAS SO AWESOME HOW WE CHASED THOSE LOSERS OUTTA THEIR FORT.
YEAH, JIMBO. WE RULE!

ONE. TWO. THREE!

WHOA, DUDES. WE'RE GOING MOBILE!

YIIIIIIII!

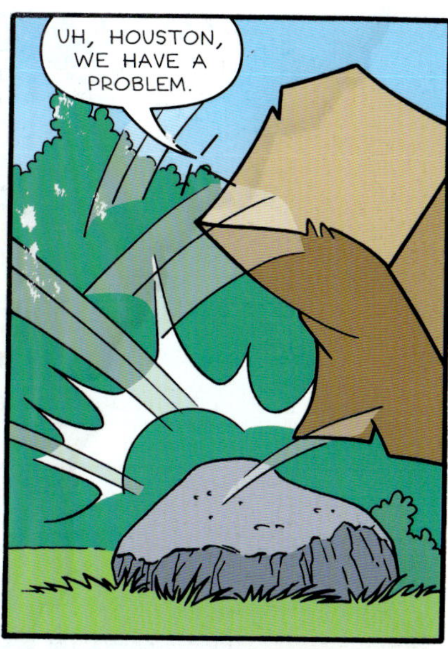
UH, HOUSTON, WE HAVE A PROBLEM.

CRASH!

THERE THEY ARE! LET'S GET 'EM!

QUICK!
IN HERE!

HEY, MILHOUSE, YOU KNOW WHAT? THIS MAKES A COOL FORT!
THE END

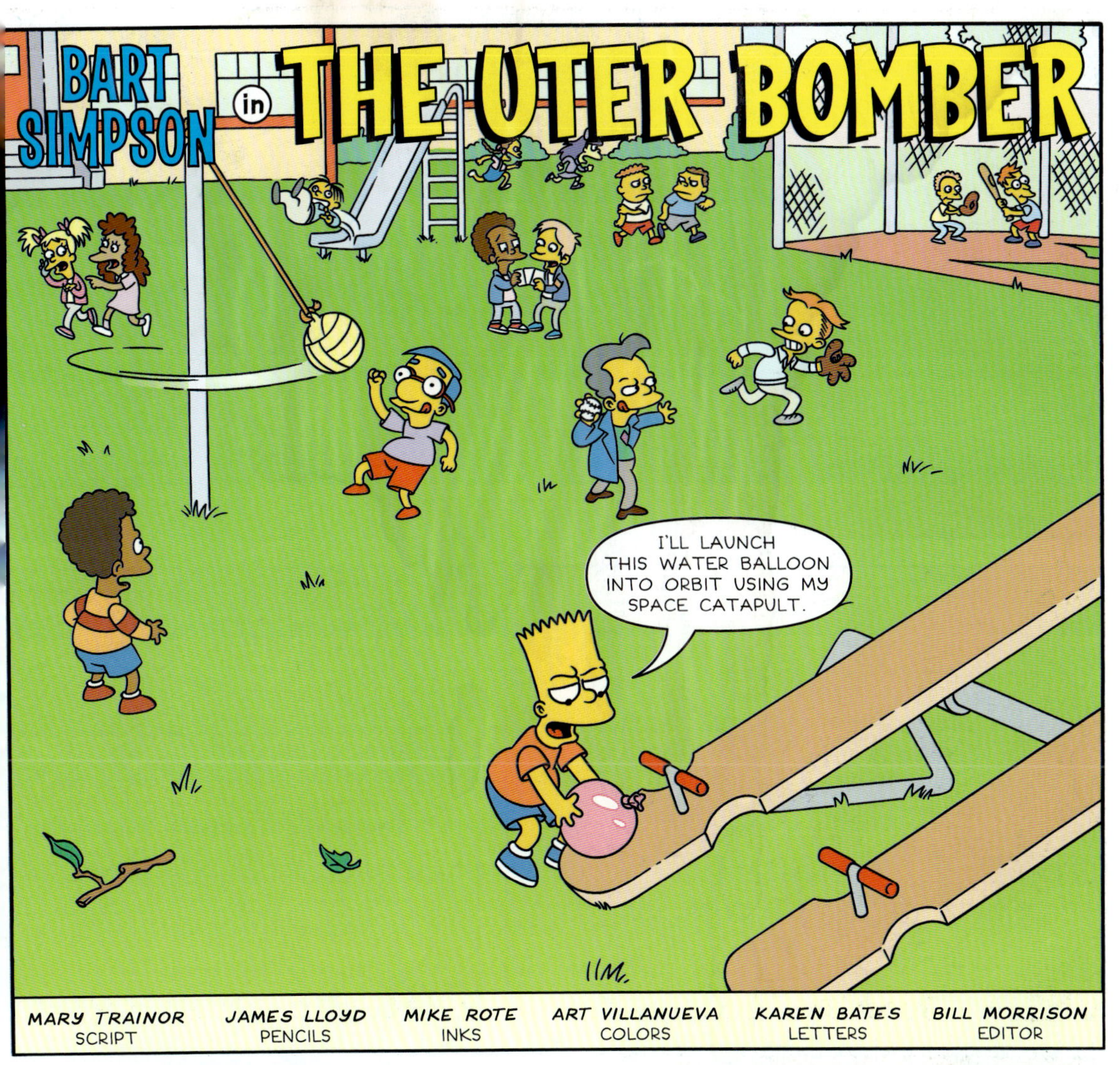
BART SIMPSON
in
THE UTER BOMBER
I'LL LAUNCH THIS WATER BALLOON INTO ORBIT USING MY SPACE CATAPULT.
MARY TRAINOR SCRIPT
JAMES LLOYD PENCILS
MIKE ROTE INKS
ART VILLANUEVA COLORS
KAREN BATES LETTERS
BILL MORRISON EDITOR

TEN...NINE... EIGHT...

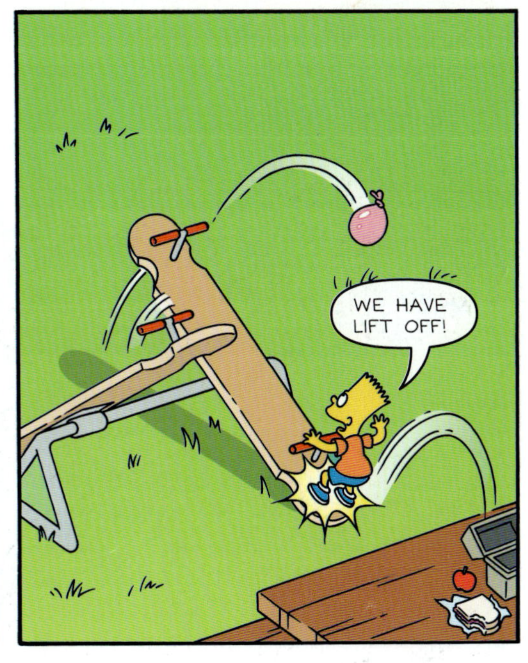
WE HAVE LIFT OFF!

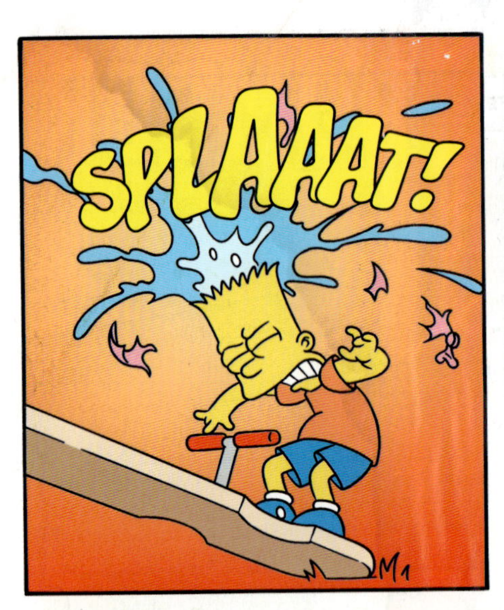
SPLAAAT!

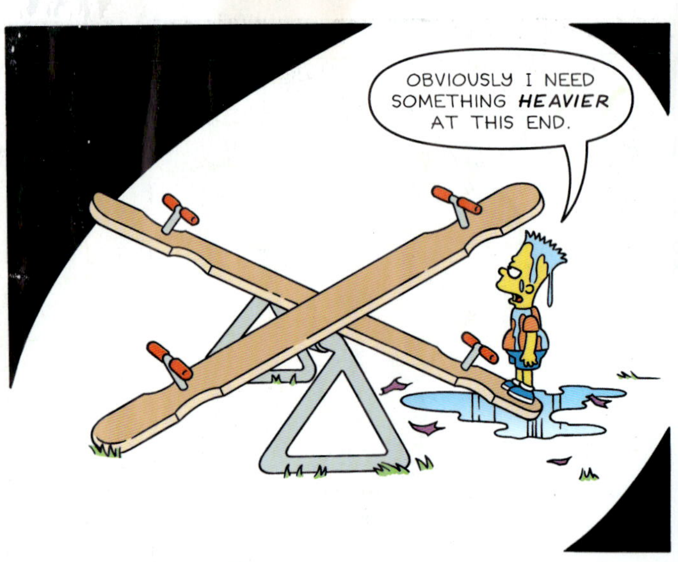
OBVIOUSLY I NEED SOMETHING HEAVIER AT THIS END.

A-HA! THE UTER BOMBER!

HEY, UTER! I'LL GIVE YOU A COOKIE IF YOU JUMP ON THIS SEESAW!

BOMBS AWAY!

OOF!

SPLAAT!
HEY!

PERFECTO!
COOKIE, PLEASE.

SURE THING, UTER.
THE HEAVIER YOU ARE, THE FARTHER THE PAYLOAD TRAVELS!

IN FACT, HAVE MY ENTIRE LUNCH!
JA! JA!

AND HAVE WENDELL'S LUNCH, TOO!
THAT'S OKAY. I WAS FEELING A LITTLE NAUSEOUS ANYWAY.

EAT UP, MY FRIEND! I'LL PREPARE THE CATAPULT FOR ANOTHER FIRING.

HI, BART! I COULDN'T HELP BUT NOTICE YOU ANALYZING THE RELATIONSHIPS AMONG FORCE, POSITION, VELOCITY AND ACCELERATION.
I WAS?

SURE. YOUR CATAPULT USES THE PHYSICS OF PROJECTILE MOTION TO LAUNCH AN OBJECT THROUGH SPACE AT A PREDETERMINED ANGLE.
IT DOES?!

NICE TO SEE YOU HAVING FUN WITH MATH!

FUN WITH MATH?!!

GAAACK!! MATH! WHY I OUGHTTA...

I'M RUNNING OUT OF THE LUNCHES, BART! WHERE ARE YOU GOING?
HEH, HEH! I JUST TOOK THE FIZZ OUT OF HIS PHYSICS!
THE END